The Best 125 Meatless Mexican Dishes

Susann Geiskopf-Hadler
and
Mindy Toomay

PRIMA PUBLISHING

Library of Congress Cataloging-in-Publication Data

Geiskopf-Hadler, Susann
 The best 125 meatless Mexican dishes / by Susann
Geiskopf-Hadler and Mindy Toomay.
  p.   cm.
 Includes index.
 ISBN 1-7615-0120-7
 1. Cookery, Mexican   2. Vegetarian cookery
 I. Toomay, Mindy.   II. Title.
TX716.M4G45   1995
641.5'636'0972—dc20   95-33223
                                                          CIP

96 97 98 99 AA 10 9 8 7 6 5 4 3 2 1

Printed in the United States of America

How to Order:
Single copies may be ordered from Prima Publishing, P.O. Box 1260BK, Rocklin, CA 95677; telephone (916) 632-4400. Quantity discounts are also available. On your letterhead, include information concerning the intended use of the books and the number of books you wish to purchase.

About the Nutritional Information:
A per serving nutritional breakdown is provided for each recipe in this book. If a range is given for the amount of an ingredient, the breakdown is based on an average of the figures given. Also, figures are rounded up or down. Nutritional content may vary depending on the specific brands or types of ingredients used. "Optional" ingredients or those for which no specific amount is stated are not included in the breakdown.

Acknowledgments

Muchas gracias to the usual suspects at Prima Publishing: Jennifer Basye Sander and Andi Reese Brady, along with Jane Gilligan, Lindy Dunlavey, and Janet Hansen. Their combined efforts have helped materialize this south-of-the-border companion to our other Best 125 books. The interior illustrations lovingly created by Miriam Davis set a warm, inviting, rustic mood that perfectly portrays the essence of Mexican cooking.

From Mindy, thanks to the late Ted Seamans—my beloved Spanish professor—and his wonderful wife—my friend—Virginia, who helped awaken a life-long passion for strong, spicy foods by introducing me to *mole poblano* at a tender age. The fire has been fueled by many cooks over the years, most notably one of my oldest and very dearest friends, Lynn Hager. Born and raised in south Texas, she grew up with the flavors of Mexico and has taught me a great deal about them. During the years we were roommates in Sacramento, our green enchilada dinner parties were legendary! I'm grateful to her for recipe inspiration and dynamic assistance in the kitchen, as well as the satisfying nourishment of her friendship. My buddy Ben Davis Jr. again stepped into the role of prep cook with skill and enthusiasm—he, too, deserves my sincere appreciation. Last but by no means least, thanks always to Tad Toomay for his dependable love and encouragement.

From Susann, thanks to my husband, Guy, who once again surrendered the kitchen and grill to me while I transported our palates to the regions of Mexico. Our travels to Mexico, as well as the Bahamas, stimulated my imagination and piqued my interest in Latin American cuisine. Thank you to the houseful of eaters who were ever present while the recipes were being developed for this book. EP Hadler, our nephew from Seattle, experienced a major culinary adventure while living with us as a freshman in college. Our nieces, Lindsey and Natalie Geiskopf, have enlivened their tender young taste buds, discovering that Mexican cuisine goes way beyond bean burritos.

Many friends graced our table, eager and willing to taste whatever I put before them. Dennis Newhall and Yvonne Shanks shared the abundance of tomatillos and epazote from their garden, and Bunnie Day and Joseph Angello contributed bushel after bushel of tomatoes from the fields around their home.

Thanks most of all to our faithful readers for adding this book to their collections.

Contents

Contents   *vii*

Almost Instant Recipes

The following list is a guide to the recipes in this book that require 30 minutes or less to prepare, from start to finish. This earns them our Almost Instant designation, which appears under the titles on the recipe pages.

Almost Instant Recipes   *xi*

Vegan Recipes

The vegan diet—which excludes meat, dairy products, and eggs—depends entirely on the nutrients found in the plant kingdom. We provide the following index of vegan recipes as a convenience for those who have embraced this approach to healthful eating.

If you plan to follow a full-time vegan diet, do your research and pay close attention to food combining to ensure proper nutrition.

Introduction

The deliciously bold cooking of Mexico is built on an ancient foundation of chiles, corn, squash, and tomatoes. These foods form the basis of a wonderfully varied cuisine that dates back at least as far as the Mayan culture of pre-Columbian times. Over the centuries, explorers and conquerors introduced many non-native crops—such as rice, beans, and onions—that thrived in the hospitable climates of Mexico and quickly became beloved ingredients.

Though these and many other foods and seasonings are enjoyed throughout Mexico, there is no single Mexican cuisine. The country covers a geographically vast area, and different regions have developed their own unique culinary traditions. We have drawn on aspects of all the cuisines of Mexico to create the recipes in this book.

The idea of vegetarian Mexican cooking takes some people by surprise. Without meat, they wonder, how is it possible to make a taco? In answer, we provide a delicious assortment of meatless taco fillings—including black beans and avocado, mushroom and corn, and spiced potatoes—along with classic or innovative renditions of many other Mexican dishes.

Cream Soup with Tequila-Sautéed Peppers and Fresh Tomatoes; Mango, Jicama, and Feta Quesadillas; Black Bean Enchiladas with Fresh Mint—these are just a few of the recipes that demonstrate the enticing potential of meatless Mexican cuisine.

We feel fortunate to live in California, where Mexican restaurants and grocery stores abound. Cooks in many other parts of the country are in luck, too, for the basic ingredients of Mexican cooking are becoming more readily available in supermarkets throughout the U.S. Those who may not have easy access to Mexican ingredients in their local communities will want to consult the list of mail-order resources on page 327.

We offer this book as a guide to the mouthwatering magic of meatless Mexican cooking. Enjoy your journey through this simple and wholesome, yet spectacular, cuisine.

Stocking
the Pantry

Mexico enjoys a warm climate and therefore a particularly long growing season, so all year long its markets are colorful with fresh produce—notably corn, tomatoes, beans, oranges, limes, squash, and of course many kinds of chiles, both fresh and dried. Southern Mexico's tropical climate makes fruits such as plantain, mango, papaya, and pineapple additional culinary mainstays.

Here we provide the information you need to stock your pantry with the ingredients important to Mexican cooking. Many of them will be available in your neighborhood supermarkets, farmers' markets, or in Mexican specialty food stores. If you don't have access to markets that provide some of the less common ingredients, you may choose to order them by mail. See page 327 for a list of mail-order resources.

Beans

Dried beans are an everyday ingredient in Mexican cooking. Two very popular beans in Mexico are pinto beans and black beans, and we call for them frequently. Also, we occasionally call for white beans and garbanzo beans. All are available, both dried and canned, at virtually every supermarket. See page 31 for general cooking instructions.

Cheeses

The recipes in this book most often call for one of three types of cheese common to Mexican cuisine.

The first type is a mild, crumbly, fresh, part-skim cheese sold in Mexico, and frequently in the U.S., as *ranchero* cheese or *queso fresco*. It is used primarily as a topping rather than a filling, since it does not melt smoothly. If unable to find ranchero cheese or queso fresco, substitute a moist, mild, not-very-salty feta. Where such a cheese is desired, our recipes may specify either "queso fresco" or "mild feta cheese."

The second type of cheese favored in Mexico is a soft one that melts well. There are many regional variations—*panela* is a common part-skim cheese that is often available in the U.S. We use panela, part-skim mozzarella, domestic Muenster, or Jack cheese in recipes where a melting cheese is desired.

The third type—*queso añejo*—is an aged cheese, much drier and saltier than queso fresco, more similar in taste and texture to Italian Romano. Romano or dry California Jack cheese make acceptable substitutes if the Mexican version cannot be located. Where such a cheese is desired, our recipes call for Romano or dry Jack.

Chiles

The cuisines of Mexico are world-renowned for their intensity and depth of flavor, achieved by skillfully combining fresh ingredients with savory and sweet seasonings. Although throughout Mexico chiles find their way into the daily diet, not all Mexican food is spicy. The pungency of chiles is often merely an undertone in a complex *mole* or salsa. And when spicy foods are served, they are accompanied by bread or fresh tortillas and a variety of condiments that bring a balance of flavors and textures to the meal.

Capsaicin is the volatile oil that gives hot chiles their heat, concentrated primarily in the internal white membrane to which the seeds are attached. Removing a chile's membranes and seeds will reduce the fire it lends to a dish. Handle fresh hot chiles such as jalapeños and serranos with care—one's skin can be burned by contact with their juice or seeds. Be especially careful not to rub your eyes or nose after handling chiles. To be on the safe side, wear thin rubber gloves while chopping hot chiles, or wash your hands with soap and water immediately afterward. Also, carefully clean your cutting board and knife.

Select fresh chiles that are glossy and succulent-looking. The stems should be firmly attached and not black or shriveled. Fresh chiles are best used immediately, but can be stored in the refrigerator wrapped in a paper towel inside a closed paper bag. As they age, the color will change from green to yellow to red. Discard overripe or mushy chiles.

Select dried chiles that are unbroken, not so dry as to be brittle, and uniformly dark in color, without any light patches that may indicate inferior quality. Dried chiles will last for several months or longer if stored in a cool, dry place.

Milk is the recommended beverage for neutralizing the effect of capsaicin, so take a few sips if you have eaten a dish that is too spicy for you.

Following is a list of chiles that are used in the recipes in this book.

Anaheim

These pale green fresh chiles are typically mild in flavor and about 5 to 6 inches in length. Also sometimes sold as California or New Mexico green chiles, they are the chiles of choice for dishes where a mild flavor is desired. For the sake of convenience, we often purchase canned mild green chiles—a popular brand is Ortega. The canned variety is already roasted and peeled.

Ancho

Anchos are dried poblano chiles, about 4 inches long, with a very dark red, wrinkled appearance. Their flavor is a combination of hot, sweet, and bitter. Many recipes specify that they be toasted, which adds a smoky note to the flavor. Other times, they are added to a recipe dry or are rehydrated in hot water. Anchos are available packaged in cellophane bags or, occasionally, loose in the produce section.

Chipotle

Chipotles are smoked jalapeños that may be purchased in dried form or, more commonly, canned *en adobo*—a sauce of tomatoes, vinegar, and spices. They have a distinctive, smoky flavor and are quite hot, so a little goes a long way. Our recipes call for chipotle chiles en adobo, since this version is available in many supermarkets and every Mexican grocery. Dried ones are more difficult to find. Once opened, transfer canned chipotles with their sauce to a glass or plastic covered container and store in the refrigerator for up to a few weeks.

Jalapeño

Fresh jalapeños, available in well-stocked supermarkets, are medium to dark green and have a somewhat rounded tip. They are typically about 2½ inches long and about ¾ inch wide and are very hot. Our recipes sometimes call for jalapeños in their pickled form—*en escabeche*—which are sold in glass jars or cans, either whole or sliced.

New Mexico

Dried New Mexico chiles are about 5 to 6 inches long and are dark rusty red with a shiny unwrinkled surface. They are a good choice when a not-too-hot red chile flavor is desired. Look for dried New Mexico chiles packaged or loose wherever Mexican ingredients are sold. Store them at room temperature in a closed, dry jar for up to several months. The dried red chiles sold as California chiles are interchangeable with New Mexico chiles.

Poblano

These dark green, almost black, chiles have a triangular shape. Fresh poblanos average 3 to 5 inches in length and 2 to 3 inches in width at the stem end. Purchase them within a few days of use as they do not keep well. Typically, poblanos are charred and peeled before being used in recipes.

Serrano

Fresh serrano chiles are bright green in color and average 2 inches in length and about ½ inch in width. They have gently pointed tips and are very hot. The serrano is our fresh chile of choice for imparting heat to Mexican dishes.

Corn

Corn is an ancient food, dating back at least to the beginnings of Aztec civilization. In Mexico and all of Latin America, corn was and is considered the food of the gods.

Fresh corn is enjoyed in a variety of dishes, but most commonly, corn is dried, then used to make masa dough. The dried corn kernels are processed with limewater (water mixed with calcium oxide), then peeled and ground to create fresh masa, ready to be made into tortillas, tamales, and other savory and sweet snacks. For longer storage, the slaked kernels are dried, then ground into a flour called *masa harina* that is reconstituted and used when fresh dough is unavailable.

Any U.S. city with a substantial Mexican population probably has a market that carries fresh masa dough. Be aware, however, that it is often made with lard and/or meat broth. Because the fresh dough can be difficult to find, and because it may contain unwanted ingredients, we have based the masa recipes in this book on convenient and easy-to-find instant masa harina. Ethnic grocery stores and many supermarkets carry it; Quaker and Maseca are two popular brands.

Slaked, peeled, and cooked corn kernels are also sold whole. This is *pozole,* known in the U.S. as hominy. It is sold canned, in both white and yellow varieties. Pozole is also available dried, but you may need to go to a well-stocked Mexican specialty store to find it.

Even the inedible part of the corn plant has its use in Mexican cuisine. See Tamale Wrappers on page 15 for information about corn husks.

Fruits

Fruits find their way into both sweet and pungent Mexican dishes. The fruits most common to Mexican cooking are discussed below.

Avocado

These rich fruits with their slightly nutty flavor are popular ingredients in Mexican cuisine. In the U.S., avocados are usually still green and unripe when they reach the supermarkets and will need to ripen for several days in a warm kitchen. We prefer the flavor and texture of Haas avocados, which are somewhat smaller than other varieties and have a bumpy, rather than smooth, skin. A perfectly ripe Haas avocado is tender, but not too soft to the touch. The pit should not move about inside when you gently shake the fruit. The skin should be attached firmly to the inside flesh, which will be dense and creamy, like firm butter. Overripe avocados are mushy, with skins that feel loose. Their interior will be discolored and stringy. Don't bother with avocado recipes unless you know you have good ripe ones on hand. Once an avocado has fully ripened, it may be stored in the refrigerator for a couple of days before using.

To remove the pit, slice the avocado in half lengthwise all the way to the pit. Using your hands, twist the two avocado halves in opposite directions. The pit will come loose from one half of the fruit. Remove the pit from the other half by hitting the pit firmly (but carefully!) with the blade of a heavy knife, imbedding the knife blade in the pit. Twist the knife to release the pit from the avocado. Scoop the flesh out of the skin, or peel and cut the fruit as specified in individual recipes.

A nutritional note: though avocados are quite high in fat, nutritional research suggests the monounsaturated variety may actually lower blood cholesterol.

Citrus Fruit

The juices of limes, lemons, and oranges are well suited to Mexican cooking. Limes, in particular, are a much favored Mexican seasoning. The limes and lemons in Mexico, we are told, are quite distinct from those commonly grown in the U.S. Where our recipes call for fresh-squeezed lime juice or lemon juice, use the standard supermarket lime and the juicy, thin-skinned Meyer lemon, if you can find it. As for oranges, the sweet Valencia is our preferred variety for juicing. We keep limes, lemons, and oranges on hand, stored in a basket at room temperature (but out of direct sunlight). They keep fairly well, becoming softer and juicier over time. Do carefully check the fruit from time to time and discard pieces that are beginning to mold.

Mango

This tropical fruit is especially popular in the cooking of the Yucatán. Mangoes are best purchased in season, from April through September. Leave unripe mangoes at room temperature for a few days. A ripe mango should be more yellow-orange or soft red than green in color, depending on the variety, and yield slightly to gentle pressure. Fully ripe mangoes will keep for several days in the refrigerator. The orange-yellow flesh is extremely juicy and very high in beta carotene. One simple method for cutting a mango is to stand it on end and slice through the flesh to the pit lengthwise in 6 places. Peel away the skin a segment at a time, then cut the flesh away from the pit. Slice or chop as needed.

Plantain

Plantains are a member of the banana family. They have a high starch content and are most commonly cooked and served as a vegetable. Larger than the common banana, they are sold while still green, but are not ready to eat until the skin has turned black and the fruit yields to gentle pressure. Ripen them in the open air at room temperature—it can take a week to 10 days before they are ready to eat. Look for plantains in markets that carry a good selection of tropical fruits.

Garlic and Onions

Mexican cuisine relies on great quantities of onions and garlic, both raw and cooked. White onions, with their astringent bite, seem to be preferred by most Mexican cooks. Our recipes typically call for white onions, but we also use yellow onions and red onions when a sweeter flavor is desired. Shallots and slender green onions are also occasionally used in this book, as they are occasionally used in Mexico. Select garlic, onions, and shallots that are firm and free of mold and sprouts. Store them in a cool dry place. Store green onions loosely wrapped in a plastic bag in the refrigerator.

Herbs and Seasonings

Every good cook's pantry—in Mexico and throughout the world—contains a wide variety of herbs and spices. But dried herbs and spices do not last indefinitely. Their volatile oils evaporate over time, diminishing their flavor. Buy dried herbs and spices in small quantities, from a bulk retailer, if possible, where quality and price are often best.

Allspice

The berry of a tropical evergreen shrub, allspice is picked green but turns dark brown when dried. Dried allspice berries lend a delicate sweet/peppery note to some Mexican dishes.

Anise

Anise seeds are a traditional ingredient in some Mexican desserts and beverages, and add an intriguing licorice-like flavor to savory foods, such as salad dressings and *moles*.

Bay Leaf

There are dozens of different varieties of bay leaves, many with culinary uses. Though the flavors they impart may be slightly different, any bay leaf sold as a seasoning is suitable in our recipes.

Chile Powder

There are many different chile powders, ranging in character from very mild paprika to searingly hot cayenne. Between these extremes, the choices are still vast. Many commercial chile powders sold in the U.S. are really a blend of spices, often including cumin and salt. Look for a product at the supermarket labeled "pure" chile powder, or buy chile powder without additional ingredients at a store that specializes in bulk herbs and spices.

Cinnamon

Mexican cooking sometimes combines hot spices with sweet ones, such as cinnamon, to create sauces with wonderful complexity. The cinnamon commonly available in the U.S. is different from the Mexican variety. Look for Mexican *canela* in an ethnic market, or substitute standard cinnamon.

Cocoa

Unsweetened cocoa is used in many sauces and *moles* throughout Mexico. It lends a mysterious richness when combined with tomatoes, cinnamon, and oregano.

Coriander

Fresh coriander, best known to U.S. cooks as cilantro and also sold as Chinese parsley, is a staple seasoning of Mexican cuisine. Buy large, leafy bunches and wrap them in paper towels before storing in a closed plastic bag in the refrigerator. Cilantro will stay fresh for several days. Wash and chop the leaves as needed. Cilantro leaves lose much of their flavor when dried, so fresh cilantro is a must in our recipes. The dried seeds of the same plant, called coriander seeds, provide a much different seasoning, which is also used in Mexican cooking, with delicious results.

Cumin

Cumin's unique pungent flavor is a common ingredient in the traditional foods of Mexico. Our recipes call for both ground and whole cumin seeds.

Epazote

This odiferous herb grows prolifically in Mexico. The fresh herb is not easy to find in the U.S., but it is easy to grow. The plants are frost sensitive, so move them indoors during the winter, or collect their seeds and replant in the early spring. Many Mexican cooks consider epazote their seasoning of choice for many dishes, black beans being a prime example. If you cannot find or grow fresh epazote, you may be able to locate it dried in Mexican groceries or well-stocked supermarkets.

Marjoram

Marjoram is a close relative of oregano, but has a more delicate floral fragrance and flavor preferred in some recipes.

Mexican Oregano

Mexican oregano has a different aroma and flavor from the Mediterranean variety most common in the U.S. Seek out the dried herb in Mexican groceries and well-stocked supermarkets. If you can't find Mexican oregano, substitute the Mediterranean variety, with slightly different but good results.

Mint

Mint grows wild throughout Mexico, as it does in much of the U.S. Where fresh mint is called for in our recipes, you may use any common garden variety, such as spearmint or peppermint.

Paprika

Mexican paprika, or *pimenton,* is sometimes available in Mexican markets in the U.S. It is complex and robust in flavor, with just a hint of sweetness. Where our recipes call for paprika, use the Mexican variety, or any sweet paprika, such as Hungarian.

Rosemary

This woody shrub yields spiky leaves with a pine-like flavor. In both fresh and dried forms, rosemary combines well with many of the foods used in Mexican cooking.

Thyme

This aromatic, versatile herb has a potent flavor compatible with other strong Mexican seasonings. Use it either fresh or dried, as specified in individual recipes.

Masa

See Corn.

Nuts and Seeds

Nuts and seeds are popular in Mexican cooking. They add richness and depth of flavor to many dishes, and are used in ground form to thicken soups and stews.

Peanuts and Almonds

These readily available nuts are common culinary ingredients in Mexico, enjoyed as snacks or added to sauces and desserts. Raw unsalted peanuts and almonds are preferred, and are available wherever bulk nuts are sold.

Pumpkins Seeds

Pumpkins seeds, or *pepitas,* have been a common ingredient in Mexican cooking since ancient times. Traditional sauces and breads are deliciously enhanced by their unique, delicate flavor. When ground, pumpkin seeds become a thickener for stews and sauces. Purchase raw unsalted pumpkin seeds at a natural food store or market that carries bulk nuts. When stored in a closed container in the refrigerator, these flat green seeds will last for many months. For best results, toast pumpkin seeds as needed.

Oils and Butter

Lard, rendered from pork, is a traditional cooking fat in Mexican kitchens. As vegetarians, we of course avoid using lard. We also prefer not to use hydrogenated solid vegetable shortening, an alternative to lard used by some cooks. The hydrogenation process transforms the more healthful unsaturated fats in vegetable oils into less desirable saturated fats. We find we can achieve excellent flavors and textures without the use of these solid fats.

Butter

We occasionally use butter in our recipes when we think its flavor will enhance a particular food. We prefer to use unsalted or "sweet" butter, which is not artificially colored, even when salt is to be added to the dish.

Canola Oil

Though some Mexican cooks consider safflower oil their oil of choice, we feel that its strong flavor can dominate certain dishes. We prefer bland canola oil in our Mexican cooking.

Infused Oils

Oil can be seasoned by soaking—or infusing—herbs, spices, and other seasonings in it. We give directions for making garlic- and rosemary-infused oils on page 36. The flavor of these special oils makes an interesting substitute for the traditional taste of lard in masa dishes.

Olive Oil

Olive oil is not the most popular oil in Mexico, perhaps because its flavor is considered too fruity. Nevertheless, we use olive oil in some recipes simply because we enjoy its taste, especially in raw dishes, such as salads.

Pasta

Pasta's place in Mexican cuisine is easily traced to early Italian immigrants. It has become an inexpensive, hearty staple in many Mexican kitchens. Our recipes call for various Italian pasta shapes, including the coiled vermicelli that is very popular in Mexico, where it is known as *fideo*. Pasta keeps indefinitely in the pantry, and we keep many different varieties on hand for quick dinner inspiration.

Rice

There is some controversy about how rice originally found its way into the cuisine of Mexico—Spain and China are quoted by differing authorities as likely sources. In any case, rice has long been established in Mexican cooking. Indeed, it is eaten almost daily by many Mexican families.

Our recipes call for either brown or white long-grain rice. Brown rice yields a more substantial, chewy texture than white, and is nutritionally superior. Often though, we prefer the lighter, more fluffy consistency of white rice. We recommend keeping brown and white varieties on hand and trying our recipes with both to find out which kind you prefer.

Stock

Chicken or pork stock are standard ingredients in traditional Mexican kitchens, but we find that vegetable stock gives excellent flavor to soups, sauces, and masa. We provide a recipe for Mexican-seasoned vegetable stock on page 38. Made-from-scratch stock has a depth of flavor far superior to that of stock made from vegetable broth cubes, though the latter may be used in a pinch. If you do use cubes, look for a low-sodium or no-salt-added variety.

Tamale Wrappers

Tamales are a popular Mexican dish made of masa dough, which is stuffed with a savory or sweet filling, then wrapped and steamed. The wrappers most frequently used are corn husks, which are available dried wherever Mexican ingredients are sold. Dried corn husks must be soaked to soften and clean them before use. Specific instructions are given with our tamale recipes.

Easy-to-locate corn husks are not, however, the only possibility for wrapping tamales. The use of banana leaves to wrap foods for steaming dates back to the Mayans. These leaves are dark in color and will tint tamales a subtle green, as well as infuse them with an interesting tropical flavor. Frozen banana leaves are available in Mexican specialty stores. Thaw them, rinse, and pat dry before using. Use scissors or a sharp knife to cut long, narrow "strings" of banana leaf to tie the finished tamales closed.

Tomatoes

Fresh tomatoes are called for in some of our sauces, salsas, and salads. For best results, make these recipes only when vine-ripened tomatoes are available. Many of our recipes call for canned tomatoes—look for brands that contain no additives.

Tortillas

See pages 158–160.

Uncommon Vegetables

We describe below the more unusual vegetables frequently used in our Mexican recipes.

Chayote

This pear-shaped summer squash most commonly has a pale green skin, although there are dark green and white varieties. The chayote has a single central seed, which is edible when cooked, and a rather thick skin. Store fresh chayotes unwrapped in the refrigerator for up to a month.

Jicama

This root vegetable is now frequently available in U.S. supermarkets, but is still unfamiliar to many cooks. Its light brown skin is stringy and should always be stripped off. A wonderful addition to salads, salsa cruda, and other raw dishes, jicama has a sweet, white flesh that maintains its delectable crispness for a long time after being cut. Jicama can run large, but purchase the smallest one available, and one that has an unblemished exterior. Jicama may be stored unwrapped for a few weeks in the refrigerator.

Nopal Cactus

Nopales (also called nopalitos) are paddles harvested from the prickly pear cactus that grow prolifically in central Mexico and is now cultivated in the Southwestern U.S. They have a succulent texture and a distinctive fresh flavor with just a hint of tartness. Nopales are available year-round. Look for them in a Mexican grocery or a well-stocked supermarket. Choose firm, unwrinkled paddles that are bright green in color. Canned nopalitos are also available, but their texture and flavor are not as good as fresh. If you do use the canned variety, be sure to drain and rinse them.

Tomatillo

Though also known as Mexican green tomatoes, tomatillos are not technically tomatoes, but rather a variety of the *Physalis* family. Tomatillos are indigenous to Mexico, yet are easy to cultivate in the warmer regions of the U.S. Their brown papery outer husks are removed before cooking, revealing a green fruit, about the size and shape of a cherry tomato. They should be rinsed thoroughly before using. Store unhusked tomatillos in a paper bag in the refrigerator for up to 2 weeks. Tomatillos are available canned; however, they tend to be overcooked and mushy, and the canning liquid has a very strong taste. Use canned tomatillos only if fresh are unavailable, and be sure to drain and rinse them.

Nutrition Alert

People who are concerned about nutrition balance their food intake based on factors beyond the outmoded "four basic food groups" concept. In 1992, the U.S. Department of Agriculture (USDA) released the Food Guide Pyramid, presenting new food groups with a different emphasis. At the base of the pyramid are the foods from which we should get most of our calories. At the tip are the foods that should supply us with the fewest calories. (To order a brochure depicting the Food Guide Pyramid and discussing the concept in detail, order Home and Garden Bulletin #252 from USDA, Human Nutrition Information Service, 6505 Belcrest Road, Hyattsville, MD 20782.)

The basic message of the pyramid is to cut down on fats and added sugars, as well as to eat a variety of foods from the different food groups. Our chief eating goals, according to the USDA, should be variety, moderation, and balance. It is the overall picture that counts; what you eat over a period of days is more important than what you eat in a single meal. A diet primarily comprised of grains and cereal products (6 to 11 servings per day), vegetables (3 to 5 servings per day), and fruits (2 to 4 servings per day), combined with lowfat protein sources (2 to 3 servings per day) and lowfat dairy products (2 to 3 servings per day) conforms to the Food Guide Pyramid, creating a well balanced mix of proteins, carbohydrates, and fats.

To some people, 3 to 5 servings of vegetables will sound like a lot, but serving sizes stipulated by the Food Guide Pyramid are moderate. A cup of leafy raw vegetables (as in a salad), ½ cup of cooked or chopped raw vegetables, or ¾ cup of vegetable juice equals 1 serving. There is no need to measure—the servings sizes are only a guideline. Furthermore, a single dish may supply servings in more than one category: for example, a sandwich may provide a grain serving (the bread), a dairy serving (the lowfat cheese), and a vegetable serving (the lettuce, sprouts, and tomato).

The nutritional experts who designed the Food Guide Pyramid recommend eating a variety of vegetables to be sure we are getting all the nutritional benefits this vast family of foods can provide. They also recommend making sure at least one serving each day is high in vitamin A; at least one each day is high in vitamin C; at least one each day is high in fiber; and that we eat cruciferous vegetables several times each week.

Vitamins A and C are particularly important because they function in the body as antioxidants. Antioxidants are a class of nutrients that neutralize "free radicals," unstable oxygen molecules that cause cell damage over time, increasing the body's vulnerability to serious disease. Vitamin A is present in animal products, or can be manufactured as needed by the body from the beta carotene in vegetables that are dark-green (for example, leafy greens and broccoli) or orange-yellow (for example, sweet potatoes). Vitamin C is present in some quantity in most fruits and vegetables—the best sources include citrus fruits, strawberries, tomatoes, broccoli, leafy greens, and sweet potatoes.

Studies have shown that antioxidants help protect us against the development of coronary heart disease and cancer, and may even slow down the aging process. Cruciferous vegetables contain considerable quantities of antioxidants, as well as beneficial nitrogen compounds called indoles, which have been shown in recent studies to be effective cancer preventers.

The Surgeon General and the American Heart Association are proponents of a semivegetarian approach to eating, which is based primarily on grains, vegetables, and fruits. The Food Guide Pyramid and other expert recommendations support semivegetarianism as an important aspect of a healthy lifestyle. The major shift required for many Americans is to view meat, if it is consumed at all, as a side dish or condiment.

Our intent here is to provide an introduction to basic nutrition. For further investigation, check with your local librarian or bookseller for comprehensive reference works.

The recipes in this book have been analyzed for calories, fat, cholesterol, sodium, carbohydrates, dietary fiber, and protein. We discuss below the importance of each of these components.

Calories

It is important to be aware of your total caloric intake in a day, but more important is to note where the calories are coming from. Calories come from three primary sources: proteins, carbohydrates, and fats. Fats contain a greater concentration of calories than do carbohydrates or proteins, and they are much harder for the body to metabolize. The U.S. Food and Drug Administration therefore suggests that the average American diet should be adjusted so that fewer calories come from fatty foods and more from carbohydrates. They specifically recommend that no more than 30 percent of the calories in our overall diets be derived from fat.

Fat

Our bodies need some fat, as it is an essential component in energy production, but it is estimated that most Americans consume six to eight times more fat than we need. High-fat diets are implicated not only in heart disease, but also in the development of some cancers, most notably of the colon and breast. Learning the basics about dietary fat is likely to contribute to a healthier—perhaps even longer—life.

The American Heart Association and the American Cancer Society recommend that a healthy adult limit calories from fat to 30 percent of total daily calories consumed. Many health professionals suggest that the fat-to-calories ratio be only 20 percent, or even 10 percent, for optimum health.

There are 9 calories in a gram of fat. A gram of protein or carbohydrate contains only 4 calories. Hence, the less fat one consumes, the lower one's intake of calories and the lower one's percentage of calories from fat. Consider that the average tablespoon of oil contains 14 grams of fat and 120 calories, while almost no fat is contained in a half cup of steamed brown rice (206 calories) or a cup of cooked broccoli (44 calories). This illustrates the volume of food that can be eaten without increasing one's fat-to-calories ratio.

To calculate the fat-to-calories ratio for a particular dish or for one's entire daily food intake, multiply the number of fat grams by 9, then divide the resulting number by the number of total calories. The result is the percentage of calories derived from fat. Keep in mind that it is okay to enjoy an occasional higher-fat dish as long as one's ratio averages 30 percent or less over the course of a day.

Another way of monitoring one's fat intake is by simply counting fat grams consumed. The nutritional analyses provided with each of our recipes facilitates this by listing fat in total grams per serving. An easy way to calculate the maximum amount of fat you should consume is to divide your body weight in half. This number is an estimate of the maximum fat in grams a moderately active, healthy adult eating a well-balanced diet could ingest over the course of a day and still maintain that weight.

Fats are divided into three categories: monounsaturated, polyunsaturated, and saturated. Saturation refers to the number of hydrogen atoms present in the fat, with saturated fats containing the most.

The primary reason to pay attention to the saturation level of fats is because diets high in saturated fats increase levels of blood cholesterol in some people—a risk factor in heart disease. Not only do monounsaturated and polyunsaturated fats not harm our hearts, they actually appear to help reduce cholesterol levels in the blood when eaten in moderation as part of an overall lowfat diet.

Therefore, it is wiser to choose foods with polyunsaturated or monounsaturated fats than with saturated fats. To make this determination, remember that most saturated fats are from animal origin and are solid at room temperature (such as butter and cheese) and most unsaturated fats are of vegetable origin and are liquid at room temperature (such as olive and canola oils).

Fiber

Dietary fiber—also called roughage—is the material from plant foods that cannot be completely digested by humans. It provides the bulk necessary to keep the digestive and eliminative systems functioning properly. Foods high in fiber also tend to be high in beta carotene, low in fat, and filling enough to reduce our dependence on higher-fat foods.

In recent years, evidence demonstrating that dietary fiber promotes human health has mounted. Studies have linked high fiber intake with reduced risk of constipation; diverticulosis;

colon, rectal, and breast cancer; heart disease; diabetes; and obesity. Because high-fiber diets tend to be low in fat and high in other health-promoting substances, it is difficult to prove their individual protective effects. However, the connection is compelling and studies are ongoing.

Many doctors now recommend adding fiber to the diet for optimum health. Organizations such as the USDA and the National Cancer Institute (NCI) have recently made increased fiber consumption part of their standard recommendations for a healthy diet.

The NCI recommends that we eat between 20 and 30 grams of fiber daily, but that our consumption not exceed 35 grams per day. Experts estimate that most Americans now eat only about half of that amount. A recent national food survey showed that diets that include five servings of fruits and vegetables daily—as recommended in the Food Guide Pyramid—provide about 17 grams of fiber. When whole grains and legumes are included in the daily diet, it's easy to reach the recommended level. Experts agree that fiber should come from foods, not supplements, which provide no nutrients. Ways to consume more fiber—along with valuable vitamins, minerals, and amino acids—include choosing whole grain rather than refined-flour products; not peeling fruits and vegetables; and eating dried peas and beans.

It is especially important for people on high-fiber diets to drink plenty of water, or the fiber can slow down or block healthy bowel functioning. Eating a great deal of fiber can cause gastrointestinal distress in people unaccustomed to it, so fiber content should be increased gradually.

Protein

Since our bodies store only small amounts of protein, it needs to be replenished daily. Although protein is needed for growth and tissue repair, it is not needed in great abundance. The National Academy of Science's Food and Nutrition Board recommends 45 grams of protein per day for the average 120-pound woman and 55 grams for the average 154-pound man.

Some nutritionists think this is more protein than people usually need. Some nutritional studies suggest, in fact, that the detrimental effects of excessive protein consumption should be of greater concern to most Americans than the threat of protein deficiency. While this debate continues, it makes sense to choose protein sources that are low in fat and, thus, calories.

Most people associate protein consumption with eating meat; however, the protein in our recipes derives from grains, legumes, and dairy products and is quite sufficient to meet the body's protein needs.

Carbohydrates

There is a common misconception that carbohydrates such as pasta, grains, and potatoes are high in calories and low in nutritive value. But starchy complex carbohydrates do not present a calorie problem; the problem is typically with the fats that are added to them.

Nutritional experts now suggest that more of our daily calories come from carbohydrates than from fats or protein, since the body provides energy more economically from carbohydrates. Carbohydrates are quickly converted into glucose, the body's main fuel.

Complex carbohydrates are low in fat and are a good source of fiber. They should comprise a large share of our daily calories.

Cholesterol

Numerous volumes have been written on cholesterol in recent years, and much is being discovered about its role in overall health and nutrition. Cholesterol is essential for the construction of cell walls, the transmission of nerve impulses, and the synthesis of important hormones. It plays a vital role in the healthy functioning of the body and poses no problem when present in the correct amount. Excess cholesterol, however, is considered a major risk factor in the development of heart disease. The U.S. Senate Select Committee on Nutrition and Human Needs recommends that the average person consume no more than 300 milligrams of cholesterol per day. The best course of action is to have your cholesterol level checked by your doctor, and follow his or her specific guidelines.

Recent studies have shown that the total amount of fat a person eats—especially saturated fat—may have more effect on the cholesterol level in the body than the actual cholesterol count found in food. Current evidence suggests that a high-fiber diet low in overall fat can reduce cholesterol levels, particularly the harmful LDL type.

Sodium

The American Heart Association recommends that sodium intake be limited to 3,000 milligrams per day (a teaspoon of salt contains 2,200 milligrams of sodium). However, the actual physiological requirement is only about 220 milligrams a day. Sodium is essential for good health, since each cell of the body must be bathed continually in a saline solution. Yet high sodium intake disrupts this balance and is associated with high blood pressure and life-threatening conditions such as heart disease, kidney disease, and stroke.

Many foods naturally contain some sodium, so you do not need to add much when cooking to achieve good flavor. Particularly if you have salt-related health concerns, dishes that taste a little bland unsalted can be seasoned with herbs or other salt-free alternatives. When our recipes call for salt, you may add less than the recommended amount, or none at all, if your doctor has advised you to drastically reduce your sodium intake.

Monitoring your intake of the above food components is important; however, unless you're under doctor's instructions, you needn't be overly rigid. It is preferable to balance your intake over the course of a day, or even several days, rather than attempting to make each meal fit a particular pattern. This approach allows you to enjoy a recipe that may be higher in fat or salt, for instance, than you would normally choose, knowing that at your next meal you can eliminate that component altogether to achieve a healthy daily balance.

The information given here is not set in stone; the science of nutrition is constantly evolving. The nutritional data for our recipes is provided for people on normal diets who want to plan healthier meals. If your physician has prescribed a special diet, check with a registered dietitian to see how these recipes fit into your guidelines.

We encourage you to spend some time learning about how foods break down and are used by the body as fuel. A basic understanding of the process and application of a few simple rules can contribute to a longer and more important—healthier life.

Seven Simple Guidelines for a Healthy Diet

1. Eat a variety of foods.
2. Maintain desirable weight.
3. Avoid too much fat, saturated fat, and cholesterol.
4. Eat foods with adequate starch and fiber.
5. Avoid excessive sugar.
6. Avoid excessive sodium.
7. If you drink alcoholic beverages, do so in moderation.

Source: National Cancer Institute, U.S. Department of Health and Human Services

An Introduction to the Recipes

Mexican cooking is an earthy art, relying more on adventurous combinations of robust ingredients than on difficult or fussy techniques. Certain techniques are essential to this bold cuisine, but they are simple to learn. The most basic are described below; others will be discussed in the Tips and Tools sections of the various chapters and in individual recipes.

A few rustic tools unique to Mexican cooking that have been around for centuries are still used today, but specialty equipment is not really required. We used conventional kitchen equipment—most notably cast-iron pans, wooden spoons, and a simple mortar and pestle—when developing these recipes.

The most sophisticated piece of modern equipment you will need to make them is a standard blender for puréeing sauces and soups.

There is one inexpensive specialty item, however, that will make your life easier if you intend to make tortillas from scratch. The tortilla press effortlessly forms a ball of masa into the appropriate pancake-like shape. A heavy, sturdy press will last a lifetime and may be made of either wood or metal. Look for one at kitchen supply stores or Mexican specialty markets.

An introduction to each chapter provides information to familiarize you with the specific categories of Mexican dishes. Please read those introductions for a comprehensive overview.

You will notice that our recipes list ingredients in an unconventional format: name of food in the first column and the quantity required in a separate column to the right. This facilitates quick perusal of the ingredients, so you can determine whether you're in the mood for that particular dish or whether you have the required foods on hand. We find this format particularly easy to follow, and hope you will agree.

General Tips for Cooking from Recipes

Follow the suggestions below to ensure a smooth and enjoyable cooking experience when working from written recipes.

- Use only the freshest, best quality ingredients. Your finished dish will be only as good as the individual components that go into it, so don't compromise on quality.

- Read a recipe all the way through before beginning to cook. This will allow you to take care of any preliminary steps, such as bringing ingredients to room temperature, and will give you a solid grasp of the entire process.

- Set out your ingredients and equipment on your work surface before you begin. This will save you walking from one end of the kitchen to the other to rummage in a cupboard for the long-lost nutmeg, for instance, while neglecting whatever is cooking on the stove.

- For certain ingredients, quantities are by nature somewhat approximate. When we call for a large carrot, for instance, the one you use may be more or less large than the one we used. This is nothing to worry about. When it is essential to the success of a dish to use a specific amount, we will provide cup or pound measurements. Otherwise, use your own judgment to decide which carrot in the bin is "large." Garlic amounts in our recipes refer to medium-size cloves. If you are using elephant garlic, or the tiny cloves at the center of a garlic bulb, adjust the number of cloves accordingly.

- Seasonings are a matter of personal taste. We have provided recipes for dishes that taste good to us, seasoned as we like them. Other people may prefer more or less of certain seasonings, such as salt or chiles. Feel free to adjust amounts to suit yourself.

- Serve hot food on warmed serving dishes and warmed individual plates so the food stays at optimal temperature as long as possible. This is easily accomplished by placing the dishes near the heat source as you cook; or warm your oven several minutes before dinnertime, turn off the heat, and place the dishes there until needed.

Techniques for the Basics

A few simple techniques that are frequently called for in our Mexican recipes are described below.

Heating Tortillas

Here are several methods for reheating homemade corn tortillas or warming up the store-bought flour or corn varieties.

1. Wrap a stack of tortillas in a heavy kitchen towel and place on a steamer rack over an inch or so of water. Cover the pot and bring to a boil over medium-high heat. Steam for about 1 minute, remove pan from the heat, and let stand for 15 to 20 minutes.

2. Heat a griddle or cast-iron skillet over medium heat and warm the tortillas, one at a time, for only 30 seconds per side. Wrap the warmed tortillas in a clean tea towel.

3. Preheat the oven to 325 degrees F. Wrap a stack of tortillas in aluminum foil and place in the oven for about 20 minutes.

4. Wrap a stack of tortillas in plastic wrap, or leave them in their original supermarket wrapping. Place in the microwave and heat on high for about 30 seconds to 1 minute, depending on your particular microwave. When heating more than a few tortillas, turn the stack over once midway through the designated time. The tortillas should be steaming hot and softened. Don't overdo it, as they can become mushy.

5. Place tortillas, one at a time, directly on the metal grate of a gas burner or on a hot grill. Heat for only 30 seconds per side. A little charring may occur, which adds good flavor. Wrap the warmed tortillas in a clean tea towel while you heat the remaining tortillas.

Cooking on a Grill

In regions where summer brings high temperatures, outdoor grilling is a great alternative to stove-top cooking, which can heat up not only the kitchen, but the entire house. In California, the climate allows us to enjoy grilled foods practically year-round.

To preheat a coal grill, start the charcoal at least 15 to 20 minutes before cooking begins so the proper temperature can be achieved in time. The grill is ready when the coals are glowing bright red and coated with a fairly thick layer of gray ash. Preheat a gas grill at least 10 minutes or according to the manufacturer's specific directions.

Some safety tips: Set up the grill in an open area away from the house, and never attempt to move a hot grill. Do not cook on a charcoal fire in high winds. Avoid wearing flowing garments when cooking on a grill. Never squirt charcoal lighter fluid directly into a fire. Use long-handled utensils and wear heavy-duty mitts. Make sure ashes are completely cold before discarding.

Cooking Beans

The texture and flavor of freshly cooked dried beans are far superior to those of canned varieties, and dried beans are economical. Where our recipes call for cooked beans, we strongly recommend you use freshly cooked ones. As a general rule, 1 cup of dried beans will yield 2 to 2½ cups of cooked beans.

Rinse dried beans thoroughly to remove surface dirt and sort them carefully. Often small dirt clods, pebbles, or other foreign objects will find their way through the factory sorters and into the market bean bins. Also discard beans that are shriveled or discolored.

We usually soak dried beans before cooking them. This softens them slightly and shortens the cooking time. Our preferred soaking method is to cover the beans with boiling water and leave them to soak, loosely covered, for at least 2 hours.

Drain off the starchy soaking liquid. Cover the beans with ample fresh water, and bring to a boil over high heat. Reduce heat to medium-low and cook until tender. Depending on the type of bean and its age, this may take anywhere from 30 minutes to 2 hours. For most uses, beans should be cooked until they yield easily to the bite, but are not mushy. If they are to be cooked further after boiling, as in a casserole, take them from the pot when barely al dente.

You may wish to add garlic, bay leaves, and/or chile flakes to the cooking water, but wait to salt the pot until the beans are tender and ready for their final seasoning, because cooking in salt can give beans a tough or rubbery texture.

Beans freeze well. Cook them in larger quantities than called for in a recipe and freeze the surplus in their cooking liquid in small measured portions.

Recipes often call for some of the bean cooking liquid in addition to the drained cooked beans, so reserve the liquid when draining the beans. Leftover bean cooking liquid can be enjoyed as a simple broth or added to soups for richness.

If you choose not to cook dried beans to use in these recipes, you may substitute canned beans. Look for a brand that does not contain additives, or drain and rinse the beans before using.

Frequently Used Homemade Ingredients

When our recipes call for ingredients such as vegetable stock or corn tortillas, you may purchase commercial varieties. For top quality and economy, however, make your own. It's easier than you think to keep homemade "convenience" foods on hand.

Mexican Crema

A slightly soured cream is often served in Mexico as a table condiment. It is neither as sour nor as thick as standard supermarket sour cream. Sometimes Mexican markets will carry crema in their dairy cases. Otherwise, you can make it at home. Here is an authentic cultured, high-butterfat crema. It takes at least 24 hours to prepare, plus chilling time, so plan ahead.

Yield: About 1 cup

Heavy whipping cream	**1 cup**
Cultured buttermilk	**2 tablespoons**

Stir the cream and buttermilk together in a glass or ceramic bowl. Cover the bowl loosely with plastic wrap and set out at room temperature, preferably where the sun will be on the bowl a good part of the day. Leave the mixture alone for 12 to 24 hours, then gently stir the mixture and transfer it to a covered jar in the refrigerator. It may not seem very thick in the bowl, but it will thicken as it chills. Use the crema immediately or over the course of about a week.

━ ━━ ━ ━━ ━ ━━ ━ ━━ ━

Each tablespoon provides:

53	Calories	1 g	Carbohydrate
0 g	Protein	9 mg	Sodium
6 g	Fat	21 mg	Cholesterol
0 g	Dietary Fiber		

Lowfat Crema

ALMOST INSTANT

This quick crema variation is more convenient and has the additional advantage of being much lower in fat than traditional crema. It can be stirred together just before using.

Yield: About 1 cup

Lowfat sour cream	**1 cup**
Nonfat milk	**3 tablespoons**

Stir together the sour cream and milk in a glass jar or plastic refrigerator container. Use immediately or refrigerate and use over the course of about a week.

Each tablespoon provides:

3	Calories	0 g	Carbohydrate
0 g	Protein	2 mg	Sodium
0 g	Fat	1 mg	Cholesterol
0 g	Dietary Fiber		

Chipotle Chile Mayonnaise

This quick-to-prepare mayonnaise has a smoky flavor that combines well with grilled foods and makes a delicious topping or dip. It can be refrigerated in a tightly closed container for up to 2 weeks. Be sure the lime juice you use is tart—not bitter.

Yield: 1½ cups

Egg*	1	**large**
Olive oil	1	**cup**
Fresh-squeezed lime juice	2	**tablespoons**
Chipotle chiles en adobo, minced	1	**tablespoon**
Salt	¼	**teaspoon**

Place the egg in a blender and process while you quickly count to 15. With the machine running, add the olive oil in a slow, steady stream. The egg and oil will emulsify into a thick sauce. Add the lime juice, chiles, and salt and process for a few seconds to incorporate. Transfer to a serving dish or a covered jar and refrigerate until ready to use.

*Some authorities suggest avoiding dishes made with raw eggs, due to the remote possibility of salmonella contamination. Immune-compromised individuals may wish to heed this advice. For further information, contact your local office of the U.S. Department of Agriculture.

— ▬ ▬ ▬ ▬ ▬ ▬ —

Each tablespoon provides:

83	Calories	0 g	Carbohydrate
0 g	Protein	29 mg	Sodium
9 g	Fat	9 mg	Cholesterol
0 g	Dietary Fiber		

Infused Oils

VEGAN

Oils infused with herbs and other seasonings can lend distinctive character to many dishes. In this book, we use garlic and rosemary oils to flavor masa dough for tamales, in place of the traditional lard or vegetable shortening. Infused oils are easy to make, but you must plan ahead since the infusion will take at least 24 hours.

Garlic Oil

Olive oil	**2**	**cups**
Garlic	**10**	**medium cloves, minced**

Combine the garlic and olive oil in a glass pint jar. Cover and allow to stand at room temperature but out of direct sunlight for 24 to 48 hours. Strain out the garlic and store the oil in a covered jar or bottle in a dark cupboard. It will keep for a few months.

———————————————

Each tablespoon provides:

113	Calories	0 g	Carbohydrate
0 g	Protein	0 mg	Sodium
13 g	Fat	0 mg	Cholesterol
0 g	Dietary Fiber		

Rosemary Oil

Olive oil	**2**	**cups**
Fresh rosemary leaves, minced	**¼**	**cup**

Place the olive oil in a glass pint jar. Rinse and carefully dry the rosemary leaves, chop them coarsely, and immerse them in the oil. Cover and allow to stand at room temperature but out of direct sunlight for 24 to 48 hours. Strain out the rosemary and store the oil in a covered jar or bottle in a dark cupboard. It will keep for a few months.

Each tablespoon provides:

113	Calories	0 g	Carbohydrate
0 g	Protein	0 mg	Sodium
13 g	Fat	0 mg	Cholesterol
0 g	Dietary Fiber		

Mexican Vegetable Stock

VEGAN

Homemade vegetable stock is a wonderful way to salvage the flavors and nutrients of vegetable trimmings. Keep a plastic bag in the refrigerator for storing items such as dried-out button mushrooms, spinach stems, and carrot trimmings, along with the stipulated fresh ingredients. Once a week, when you are at home for a couple hours, boil up a batch of stock using the saved vegetable trimmings and the stipulated fresh ingredients. Allow to cool and then freeze in 2-cup containers for future use. Of course, you may also use whole fresh vegetables to make stock. If stock-making is not a habit you're likely to develop, keep vegetable broth cubes on hand to make instant stock when needed. For best results, look for a no-salt-added or low-sodium variety. But we strongly encourage you to try making your own!

Yield: About 10 cups

Russet potatoes	2	**medium**
Onions (any color)	2	**medium, coarsely chopped**
Garlic	3	**cloves, crushed but not peeled**
Celery, coarsely chopped	2	**cups**
Button mushrooms, chopped	2	**cups**
Mixed chopped fresh vegetables and trimmings	4	**cups**
Fresh cilantro, chopped	¼	**cup**
Bay leaves	2	
Dried Mexican oregano	2	**teaspoons**
Cumin seeds	1	**teaspoon, crushed**
Dried thyme	½	**teaspoon**
Dried red chile flakes	¼	**teaspoon**
Salt	¼	**teaspoon**

Put 16 cups of water in a stockpot over high heat. Scrub the potatoes but do not peel them. Chop them coarsely and add to the water along with all the remaining ingredients. Bring to a boil over high heat, then reduce the heat to medium and simmer, uncovered, for 45 minutes. Turn off the heat and allow the mixture to steep an additional 15 to 30 minutes before straining into glass jars, leaving 1 inch of headroom. Cool, cover, and refrigerate for up to a week, or freeze for longer storage.

Each cup provides:

10	Calories	2 g	Carbohydrate
1 g	Protein	52 mg	Sodium
0 g	Fat	0 mg	Cholesterol
0 g	Dietary Fiber		

Tofu Chorizo Sausage

VEGAN

Many people who have traveled in Mexico fondly recall the potent flavor of chorizo. This simple recipe will convince you that the flavor of chorizo is mostly in the seasoning, not in the pork traditionally used to make the spicy sausage. In this meatless version, ancho chiles, garlic, and an abundance of other strong seasonings create a mouthwatering intensity of flavor, and long cooking over high heat creates a satisfying chewy texture. Use the resulting mixture as a Mexican cook would, stirred into scrambled eggs (page 251) or as a filling for tacos (page 178) or sopes (page 222). Allow ample time to drain the tofu before the cooking begins.

Yield: 3 cups

Firm tofu	1	**pound**
Dried ancho chiles	3	**large**
Garlic	4	**cloves, chopped**
Dried Mexican oregano	1	**tablespoon**
Paprika	2	**teaspoons**
Cumin seeds	1½	**teaspoons**
Salt	1	**teaspoon**
Dried red chile flakes	⅛	**teaspoon**
Whole cloves	4	
Cinnamon stick	1	**piece (¼ inch)**
Apple cider vinegar	2	**tablespoons**
Smooth peanut butter	2	**tablespoons**
Mexican Vegetable Stock*	1¼	**cups**

*If you do not have Mexican Vegetable Stock on hand, make a batch according to the directions on page 38, or dissolve ½ of a large low-sodium vegetable broth cube in 1¼ cups hot water.

Cut the tofu into ½-inch-thick slices and place the slices on a clean tea towel. Cover with another clean tea towel and place a baking sheet on top. Place a weight (jars of beans work well) on the baking sheet so the tofu is firmly pressed between the towels. Allow the tofu to drain in this manner for a few hours to remove as much water as possible.

Meanwhile, heat a cast-iron griddle or heavy-bottomed skillet over medium-high heat. Use your hands to tear the chiles into large pieces, discarding the stems and seeds. Place the chile pieces on the hot griddle and toast for 1 to 2 minutes, occasionally pressing down on them with a metal spatula. They should blister a bit and begin to lighten in color. Turn them over and toast the other side briefly.

When the chiles are lightly toasted, place them in a food processor with the garlic, oregano, paprika, cumin seeds, salt, chile flakes, cloves, and cinnamon stick. Process until finely ground. Add the vinegar, peanut butter, and ¼ cup of the stock and purée to a smooth consistency. Add the remaining 1 cup stock and purée briefly, then transfer the mixture to a heavy-bottomed skillet. Crumble the tofu pieces into the skillet.

Heat over medium-high until the sauce begins to simmer. Reduce the heat to medium-low and cook for about 20 minutes, frequently stirring and scraping the bottom and sides of the skillet with a metal spatula to incorporate any stuck bits of tofu. The chorizo is done when the tofu has a fairly dry, crumbly consistency. Use immediately, or store for up to a few days in a covered container in the refrigerator.

Each cup provides:

258	Calories	18 g	Carbohydrate
15 g	Protein	794 mg	Sodium
17 g	Fat	0 mg	Cholesterol
3 g	Dietary Fiber		

Fresh Corn Tortillas

ALMOST INSTANT, VEGAN

This recipe carries the distinction of having the shortest ingredient list of any recipe we've ever published. How difficult could it be? Fresh tortillas are quick and easy to make from instant masa harina, which is sold under various brand names in North American supermarkets. Maseca and Quaker are common brands. In Mexico, experienced cooks pat out perfectly thin and round tortillas between their hands. We like to use the convenient tortilla press, as described in detail below. A rolling pin can also be used to roll out the dough balls. By all means, buy a bag of inexpensive masa harina and have fun experimenting with tortillas and other traditional masa dishes (see Tamales and Other Masa Dishes, page 202).

Yield: 12 tortillas

Instant masa harina	**2 cups**

In a medium bowl, use your hands to combine the masa harina with $1\frac{1}{4}$ cups lukewarm water. Work the mixture together until all the water is incorporated and you have a nice moist dough, then continue to work it for 1 to 2 minutes. If the dough is dry and crumbly, add additional lukewarm water, 1 tablespoon at a time, to correct the texture. If it is too wet and sticky, add additional masa harina, 1 tablespoon at a time. You want a dough that holds together well but is not overly sticky.

Preheat a cast-iron griddle or heavy-bottomed skillet over medium heat for at least 5 minutes. Have a spatula at the ready. Place a sheet of waxed paper or plastic wrap on a wooden tortilla press, or insert the plastic part that comes with the metal presses. Pinch off a dough ball about the size of a large walnut, about one twelfth of the dough, and roll it in your hands to make a fairly round shape. Cover the remaining dough with a clean tea towel or plastic wrap to prevent it from drying out. Place the ball in the center of the tortilla press and top with another sheet of waxed paper.

Close the press, using a vigorous pressing motion to flatten out the ball. Peel off the top sheet of waxed paper and transfer the peeled side of the tortilla to your hand. Peel off the other waxed paper and slap the tortilla gently onto the hot griddle. (If the paper will not peel easily from the tortilla, the dough is too wet. Scrape the dough back into the bowl and work in a bit more masa harina until the proper consistency is achieved. If the edge of the tortilla shows large cracks, the dough is too dry. Return the dough to the bowl and work in a bit more water until the proper consistency is achieved.)

Place the tortilla on the preheated griddle and cook for about 30 seconds on one side. Turn it over and cook for about 1 minute, then turn again and cook for 1 more minute. It is fine if the tortilla puffs up during the cooking time. The cooked tortilla should be barely flecked with brown, toasted spots. Wrap the cooked tortilla in a clean tea towel. Proceed in this fashion until you have cooked all 12 tortillas. Serve immediately or use in your favorite recipe.

Cooked tortillas may be wrapped in plastic wrap or aluminum foil and stored in the refrigerator for a day or two. Reheat them as described on page 30.

Each tortilla provides:

71	Calories	15 g	Carbohydrate
2 g	Protein	2 mg	Sodium
1 g	Fat	0 mg	Cholesterol
1 g	Dietary Fiber		

Table Salsas
and Condiments

The terminology for the varied sauces of Mexico can be confusing. The term *salsa* may be applied to cooked as well as raw sauces, to the chunky as well as the smooth. For our purposes, however, we define salsa as an uncooked condiment. In Mexico, more than one salsa frequently appears on the table at each meal, to be spooned on top of other foods in combinations dictated by the tastes of each diner.

Most of the salsas in this chapter are mild enough to be enjoyed by the whole family, though a few are sufficiently spicy to satisfy hot chile lovers.

Salsas keep well. In fact, many will improve over the course of several days if stored in a covered container in the refrigerator. Home canners may make their favorite salsas in large quantities, putting them up in pint jars to be enjoyed throughout the year.

Among the following recipes, we hope you discover at least a few favorites.

Tips and Tools

- For the best flavor, make the salsas several hours before they are to be served. Hold them at room temperature to allow the flavors to develop.

- Store leftover salsa in a covered container in the refrigerator for up to several days, but return to room temperature before serving, if possible.

- A very sharp knife and thin rubber gloves will facilitate the seeding and mincing of hot chiles.

Black Bean and Corn Salsa with Serrano Chiles and Lime Juice

ALMOST INSTANT, VEGAN

This is a great salsa to prepare any time of the year, but we especially like it made with the crunch of summer's sweet, fresh corn kernels. Serve this colorful salsa with chips or crisp vegetables.

Yield: 5 cups

Serrano chiles	2	small
Cooked black beans*	3½	cups, drained
Corn kernels, fresh or frozen**	2	cups
Red bell pepper	1	medium
Fresh-squeezed lime juice	¼	cup
Olive oil	1	tablespoon
Ground cumin	¼	teaspoon
Granulated garlic	½	teaspoon
Pure chile powder	½	teaspoon

Remove and discard the stems of the chiles and scrape out the seeds and membrane for a milder salsa. Finely mince the chiles and set aside briefly.

Toss the beans and corn together in a large bowl. Remove and discard the stem, seeds, and membrane of the red bell pepper. Dice the pepper and add it to the beans and corn, along with the chiles. Toss to combine.

*Cook dried beans according to the instructions on page 31, or purchase canned beans that do not contain additives.

**If you are using fresh corn, you will need about 4 medium ears to yield 2 cups kernels.

Whisk together the lime juice, olive oil, cumin, garlic, and chile powder. Pour over the bean mixture and toss to combine. Cover and set aside at room temperature for at least 15 minutes before serving.

Each 2-tablespoon serving provides:

16	Calories	3 g	Carbohydrate
1 g	Protein	1 mg	Sodium
0 g	Fat	0 mg	Cholesterol
1 g	Dietary Fiber		

Tomatillo Salsa with Red Tomatoes and Zucchini

ALMOST INSTANT, VEGAN

The tomatillo is native to central Mexico, although this prolific plant is easy to cultivate in any warm climate. It has a slightly lemon-like flavor and a crisp texture when raw. We enjoy this salsa with grilled foods, poached eggs, or just tortilla chips.

Yield: 4 cups

Fresh tomatillos	½	**pound (6 medium)**
Fresh tomatoes	2	**medium (about 1 pound)**
Fresh zucchini, diced	¾	**cup (1 medium)**
Red onion, diced	½	**cup**
Canola oil	1	**tablespoon**
Fresh-squeezed lemon juice	1	**tablespoon**
Garlic	2	**cloves, minced**
Dried Mexican oregano	1	**teaspoon**
Ground cumin	½	**teaspoon**
Cayenne		**Scant ⅛ teaspoon**
Salt	⅛	**teaspoon**
Black pepper		**Several grinds**

Remove and discard the husks of the tomatillos. Rinse and dice them, and set aside in a bowl. Cut the tomatoes in half crosswise and gently squeeze over the sink to remove the juicy seed pockets. Cut out the stem ends and dice the tomatoes into uniform pieces. Add the tomatoes, zucchini, and red onion to the bowl.

In a separate bowl, whisk together the oil, lemon juice, garlic, oregano, cumin, cayenne, salt, and pepper. Pour over the vegetables and toss well. Serve immediately, or allow the flavors to blend at room temperature for about 30 minutes before serving.

■■ ■■■■ ■■ ■■■■ ■■ ■■■■ ■■ ■■■■ ■

Each 2-tablespoon serving provides:

10	Calories	1 g	Carbohydrate
0 g	Protein	9 mg	Sodium
1 g	Fat	0 mg	Cholesterol
0 g	Dietary Fiber		

Green Tomato Salsa with Poblano Chiles

ALMOST INSTANT, VEGAN

This is a great way to use up late summer green tomatoes. The recipe yields a generous amount that will stay fresh in the refrigerator for a week or so, or put up extra salsa in sterilized canning jars and process in a hot water bath for 15 minutes. We especially enjoy the flavors of this salsa with black beans and quesadillas.

Yield: 12 cups

Fresh poblano chiles	2	large (about ½ pound)
Cumin seeds	½	teaspoon
Green tomatoes	2½	pounds
Yellow onion	1	medium, diced
Red bell pepper	1	medium, diced
Fresh-squeezed lemon juice	¼	cup
Garlic	3	cloves, minced
Salt	1	teaspoon
Black pepper	¼	teaspoon
Dried red chile flakes	¼	teaspoon
Fresh cilantro leaves, minced	⅓	cup

Roast the poblano chiles on a hot grill or under the broiler for about 5 minutes, or until the skin is uniformly charred. Turn and blacken the other side. Place them in a paper or plastic bag, close the bag, and set aside at room temperature; the steam inside the bag will finish cooking the chiles.

Cut out and discard the stem ends of the green tomatoes. Without peeling them, dice the tomatoes and place them in a large bowl. Add the onion and red bell pepper, tossing to combine. When the roasted peppers are cool enough to handle, remove the skins, discard the stems and seeds, and dice the pulp. Combine with the tomato mixture.

Crush the cumin seeds with a mortar and pestle. Place the lemon juice, garlic, salt, cumin seeds, pepper, and chile flakes in a small bowl and whisk together. Pour over the green tomato mixture and toss to combine. Add the cilantro and toss again. Serve immediately or set aside at room temperature for 30 minutes or so before serving to allow the flavors to blend.

━━━━━━━━━━━━━━

Each 2-tablespoon serving provides:

5	Calories	1 g	Carbohydrate
0 g	Protein	25 mg	Sodium
0 g	Fat	0 mg	Cholesterol
0 g	Dietary Fiber		

Tomato, Fresh Corn, and Cilantro Salsa

ALMOST INSTANT, VEGAN

This is one of our all-time favorite salsas. If you know how to can foods, make a few batches to pack into pint jars so you can enjoy this salsa year-round. Sweet white corn is preferred in this recipe, but the yellow variety is also good.

Yield: 6 cups

Fresh pear tomatoes	1½	**pounds**
Canned diced mild green chiles	1	**4-ounce can**
Fresh corn kernels	¾	**cup (about 1 large ear)**
Fresh cilantro leaves, minced	½	**cup**
White vinegar	2	**tablespoons**
Olive oil	1	**tablespoon**
Granulated garlic	½	**teaspoon**
Pure chile powder	½	**teaspoon**
Ground cumin	¼	**teaspoon**

Cut out and discard the stem ends of the tomatoes; it is not necessary to peel them. Dice the tomatoes and combine with the chiles, corn, and cilantro in a medium bowl.

Whisk together the vinegar, olive oil, garlic, chile powder, and cumin, then pour over the tomato mixture. Serve immediately or set aside at room temperature for about 30 minutes to allow the flavors to blend.

Each 2-tablespoon serving provides:

9	Calories	1 g	Carbohydrate
0 g	Protein	22 mg	Sodium
0 g	Fat	0 mg	Cholesterol
0 g	Dietary Fiber		

Salsa Cruda

ALMOST INSTANT, VEGAN

This fresh table salsa is made with tomatoes that are raw, or cruda. The tomatoes must be very ripe but not mushy. This is the perfect salsa for summer, when tomatoes are at their peak of flavor.

Yield: 5 cups

Fresh jalapeño chiles	2	**medium**
Fresh tomatoes, very ripe	2½	**pounds**
Fresh-squeezed lime juice	3	**tablespoons**
White onion	1	**medium, finely diced**
Fresh cilantro leaves, minced	½	**cup**
Green onions	2	**medium, minced**
Garlic	2	**cloves, minced**
Pure chile powder	2	**teaspoons**
Salt	¼	**teaspoon**
Black pepper		**A few grinds**

Remove and discard the stems of the chiles and scrape out the seeds and membrane for a milder salsa. Finely mince the chiles and place them in a large bowl. Cut the tomatoes in half crosswise and gently squeeze over the sink to remove the juicy seed pockets. Without peeling them, dice the tomatoes and add them to the bowl. Add the remaining ingredients and stir to combine thoroughly. Use what you need immediately and store the remainder in a tightly closed container in the refrigerator for up to a week.

Each 2-tablespoon serving provides:

10	Calories	2 g	Carbohydrate
0 g	Protein	18 mg	Sodium
0 g	Fat	0 mg	Cholesterol
1 g	Dietary Fiber		

Salsa Fresca

ALMOST INSTANT, VEGAN

For the sake of convenience, this recipe calls for canned green chiles. You may substitute 5 fresh Anaheim chiles that have been roasted and peeled, if you wish. The flavor of this simple salsa does improve over time, but you may eat it immediately. Store any extra salsa in the refrigerator for several days in a tightly closed container. If you are accustomed to canning foods, this recipe may be made in larger quantities and put up for the pantry.

Yield: 5 cups

Fresh pear tomatoes	**2½**	**pounds**
Canned whole mild green chiles	**1**	**7-ounce can**
Fresh-squeezed lemon juice	**¼**	**cup**
White onion, minced	**½**	**cup**
Fresh cilantro leaves, minced	**⅓**	**cup**
Garlic	**2**	**cloves, minced**
Salt	**⅛**	**teaspoon**
Black pepper		**A few grinds**

Blanch the tomatoes by immersing them in rapidly boiling water for 2 to 3 minutes. Meanwhile, fill a large bowl or basin with ice water. Drain the tomatoes in a colander and immediately plunge them into the ice water. When they are cool enough to handle, peel the tomatoes. Remove and discard the stem ends and cut the tomatoes in half crosswise. Gently squeeze over the sink to remove the juicy seed pockets, then dice the tomatoes and place them in a bowl. Drain off any juice that collects in the bowl.

Drain the liquid from the canned green chiles and chop them finely. Add them to the tomatoes, along with the remaining ingredients. Toss gently to combine well. Serve immediately or refrigerate until needed.

Each 2-tablespoon serving provides:

8	Calories	2 g	Carbohydrate
0 g	Protein	48 mg	Sodium
0 g	Fat	0 mg	Cholesterol
0 g	Dietary Fiber		

Smooth Tomatillo Salsa

ALMOST INSTANT, VEGAN

This table salsa is delicious with chips, raw or grilled vegetables, and scrambled eggs. It is easy to make and may be refrigerated for several days. For a milder sauce, remove the seeds of the pickled jalapeños.

Yield: 2 cups

Fresh tomatillos	1	**pound (12 medium)**
White onion, minced	¼	**cup**
Fresh cilantro leaves, minced	¼	**cup**
Fresh-squeezed lime juice	1	**tablespoon**
Pickled jalapeño chiles, minced	1	**tablespoon**
Garlic	2	**cloves, minced**
Salt	¼	**teaspoon**

Remove and discard the husks of the tomatillos. Rinse the tomatillos and place them in a saucepan. Cover with water, and bring to a boil over high heat. Cover the pan, reduce the heat to medium and simmer for about 10 minutes, until the tomatillos are very tender. Drain the tomatillos and place them in a food processor. Pulse to chop, then add the onion, cilantro, lime juice, chile, garlic, and salt. Purée until smooth.

Transfer to a serving bowl and serve immediately, or refrigerate for up to several days. The salsa will thicken to a jelly-like consistency when refrigerated, but will liquefy when brought back to room temperature, or can be thinned with a bit of water or beer.

————————————————

Each 1-tablespoon serving provides:

5	Calories	1 g	Carbohydrate
0 g	Protein	23 mg	Sodium
0 g	Fat	0 mg	Cholesterol
0 g	Dietary Fiber		

Smooth Chipotle Chile Salsa

ALMOST INSTANT, VEGAN

Medium-hot on the spicy scale, this simple salsa is made with chipotle chiles canned in adobo sauce, which are available in most supermarkets. As with all puréed salsas, this one can be enjoyed immediately or will improve in a covered container in the refrigerator over the course of a week or longer.

Yield: 1¾ cups

Canned tomatoes, chopped and drained	1	**cup**
White onion, diced	⅔	**cup**
Tomato paste	2	**tablespoons**
Fresh-squeezed lime juice	1	**tablespoon**
Chipotle chiles en adobo	2	**medium**
Adobo sauce from canned chipotle chiles	2	**teaspoons**
Ground cumin	2	**teaspoons**
Garlic	2	**cloves**

Combine all the ingredients in a blender or food processor and purée to a smooth consistency. Serve immediately, or set aside at room temperature for a few hours so the flavors can blend. The sauce can be refrigerated for a week or so. It will thicken to a jelly-like consistency when refrigerated, but will liquefy when brought back to room temperature, or can be thinned with a bit of water or beer.

Each 1-tablespoon serving provides:

2	Calories	0 g	Carbohydrate
0 g	Protein	10 mg	Sodium
0 g	Fat	0 mg	Cholesterol
0 g	Dietary Fiber		

Smooth Ancho Chile Salsa

ALMOST INSTANT, VEGAN

This thick, rich salsa is a consistent favorite. It is quite simple to prepare and is a perfect pungent condiment to serve with almost any Mexican entrée.

Yield: 1½ cups

Dried ancho chiles	2	**medium**
Canned tomatoes, drained and chopped	¾	**cup**
White onion, diced	½	**cup**
Fresh cilantro leaves, minced	¼	**cup**
Garlic	1	**clove**
Fresh-squeezed lime juice	2	**teaspoons**
Ground cumin	1	**teaspoon**
Salt	⅛	**teaspoon**

Heat a cast-iron griddle or heavy-bottomed skillet over medium-high heat. Use your hands to tear the chiles into large pieces, discarding the seeds and stems. Place the chile pieces on the hot griddle and toast them for 1 to 2 minutes, occasionally pressing down on them with a metal spatula. They should blister a bit and begin to lighten in color. Turn them over and briefly toast the other side.

When the chiles are toasted, place them in a food processor along with the remaining ingredients. Purée to a smooth consistency. Serve immediately or allow to stand at room temperature for a few hours so the flavors can blend. The sauce will keep for about a week in a tightly closed container in the refrigerator, but return it to room temperature before serving.

─────────────────────────

Each 1-tablespoon serving provides:

2	Calories	1 g	Carbohydrate
0 g	Protein	8 mg	Sodium
0 g	Fat	0 mg	Cholesterol
0 g	Dietary Fiber		

Smooth Cilantro Salsa

ALMOST INSTANT, VEGAN

This thin purée can spark up any number of dishes. It is particularly good with potatoes, beans, and eggs. It also makes a great dip for tortilla chips.

Yield: ¼ cup

Fresh cilantro leaves	1	**cup**
Olive oil	2	**tablespoons**
Fresh-squeezed lemon juice	2	**teaspoons**
Ground coriander	¼	**teaspoon**
Pure chile powder	⅛	**teaspoon**
Salt		**A pinch**

Place the cilantro in a food processor and pulse to chop. Whisk together the olive oil, lemon juice, coriander, chile powder, and salt. Add to the cilantro and purée. Serve immediately or set aside at room temperature for a few hours so the flavors can blend.

━ ━━ ━ ━━ ━ ━━ ━ ━━ ━

Each 1½-teaspoon serving provides:

31	Calories	0 g	Carbohydrate
0 g	Protein	5 mg	Sodium
3 g	Fat	0 mg	Cholesterol
0 g	Dietary Fiber		

Onion, Cilantro, and Serrano Relish

ALMOST INSTANT, VEGAN

*Here is a delicious, spicy, and crunchy topping for tostadas and tacos.
Serve as a condiment along with more conventional tomato-based
salsas. Cilantro fans will be wild about it! If you like your salsa* muy
picante *(very hot), do not remove the seeds of the chiles.*

Yield: 2 cups

Fresh serrano chiles	**2**	**medium**
White onion, minced	**1¼**	**cups**
Fresh cilantro leaves, minced	**1**	**cup**
Fresh-squeezed lime juice	**2**	**tablespoons**
Salt	**¼**	**teaspoon**

Remove and discard the stems of the chiles and scrape out the
seeds for a milder relish. Finely mince the chiles. In a serving
bowl, stir the chiles together with the onion, cilantro, lime juice,
and salt until well combined. Serve immediately, or cover the
dish and allow the mixture to stand at room temperature for a
few hours before serving. Leftovers will keep well in a covered
container in the refrigerator.

Each 2-tablespoon serving provides:

8	Calories	2 g	Carbohydrate
0 g	Protein	36 mg	Sodium
0 g	Fat	0 mg	Cholesterol
0 g	Dietary Fiber		

Pickled Vegetables and Serrano Chiles with Oregano and Thyme

VEGAN

*The people of Mexico enjoy vegetables pickled in brine, or
en escabeche, and frequently include a bowl of them on the table
as a condiment. They also work well as an appetizer (about ½ cup
per person) when served with other savory tidbits. The pickled
vegetables can be refrigerated and enjoyed over the course of
several weeks.*

Yield: 14 cups

White onions	1	**pound**
Carrots	½	**pound**
Green beans	½	**pound**
Fresh cauliflower, chopped	4	**cups (1 pound)**
Garlic	20	**medium cloves**
Fresh serrano chiles	10	**medium**
Black peppercorns	1	**tablespoon, crushed**
Bay leaves	3	
Salt	1½	**teaspoons**
Dried Mexican oregano	1	**tablespoon**
Dried thyme	1	**teaspoon**
White vinegar	3	**cups**
Extra-virgin olive oil	½	**cup**

Peel the onions and cut them lengthwise into 1-inch wedges.
Place them in a large nonmetallic bowl, crock, or gallon jar.
Bring a few quarts of water to a boil in a large stockpot. Scrub
and thinly slice the carrots. Trim off the stem ends of the beans
and string them, if necessary. Cut them in half crosswise.

When the water is boiling, drop in the carrots, beans, cauliflower, unpeeled garlic cloves, and chiles. When the water returns to a boil, set your timer for 3 minutes. When it rings, immediately drain the vegetables, rinsing them with cold water to stop the cooking. Add the well-drained vegetables to the onions in the bowl, along with the peppercorns, bay leaves, salt, oregano, and thyme and stir to combine well.

In a medium saucepan, bring the vinegar to the steaming stage, along with 4 cups of water. Remove the saucepan from the heat and whisk in the olive oil. Immediately pour over the vegetables and seasonings. Add more vinegar, if necessary, so that the contents of the bowl are entirely submerged. Stir to combine, cover the bowl with a plate or board, and allow to stand at room temperature but out of direct sunlight, stirring at least once a day, for up to 4 days. You may eat from the bowl any time you wish. After 4 days, any remaining vegetables should be refrigerated.

■━━ ━━ ━━━ ━━ ━━ ━ ━━ ━

Each ½-cup serving provides:

33	Calories	6 g	Carbohydrate
1 g	Protein	30 mg	Sodium
1 g	Fat	0 mg	Cholesterol
2 g	Dietary Fiber		

Appetizers

The people of Mexico are quite fond of snacks, as demonstrated by the abundance of street vendors in towns and villages, the tidbits that always appear with drinks at a cantina, and the tantalizing array of finger foods that appear at gala family gatherings.

Creative, colorful, and encompassing many different tastes and textures, these *antojitos* (literally, little whims) may be as simple as seasoned sliced jicama or classic guacamole. Others are more elaborate but well worth the trouble, such as the delicious filled turnovers called empanadas.

These more substantial antojitos are delicious served as a lunch or light supper, perhaps accompanied by beans, rice, and salad, and, of course, an array of condiments and table salsas.

Tips and Tools

- Supermarkets carry a wide variety of tortilla chips. Taste several brands of chips to discover one that is crisp without being oily, and flavorful but not too salty. In Mexico, most home cooks make their own chips from fresh or stale tortillas. If you want to try this, be sure the frying oil is very hot before adding the tortilla triangles, so they will not soak up excessive oil.

- A traditional quesadilla is made from fresh corn tortillas, which are stuffed, folded like a turnover, and deep-fried in oil. We prefer our quesadillas made with flour tortillas and toasted in a dry skillet instead. Made this way, they are lighter and not crumbly crisp.

- A well-seasoned cast-iron skillet or griddle is one of every cook's most treasured tools. It can withstand very high temperatures and requires very little or no oil for heating tortillas, quesadillas, and the like. We have collected various sizes over the years for optimal versatility.

- Colorful earthenware bowls and platters are particularly appropriate for serving Mexican appetizers.

Empanadas with Savory Plantain Filling

These small pastry turnovers are a wonderful appetizer. The plantain filling is savory and slightly sweet—a combination typically found in the Caribbean regions of Mexico. Be sure to buy the plantain a week to 10 days in advance so it can ripen (see page 8). The empanadas also may be served as a light entrée with Romaine and Radish Salad with Orange Anise Dressing (page 124).

Yield: 12 empanadas

The pastry

Unbleached flour	1¼	cups
Fine yellow cornmeal	⅓	cup
Baking powder	1½	teaspoons
Salt	½	teaspoon
Unsalted butter	2	tablespoons

The filling

Fresh pear tomatoes	½	pound
Canola oil	1	tablespoon
White onion, minced	½	cup
Garlic	3	cloves, minced
Black pepper		Several grinds
Ground cinnamon	¼	teaspoon
Ground cloves		A pinch
Raisins	¼	cup
Water-packed green olives, pitted and minced	½	cup
Fresh ripe plantain	1	large
Unsalted butter	1	tablespoon

To make the pastry, blend together the flour, cornmeal, baking powder, and salt in a large bowl. Using a pastry cutter or food processor, cut the butter into the dry ingredients until the mixture resembles fine bread crumbs. Drizzle ⅓ cup of cold water over the surface and cut it in with the pastry cutter or food processor to form a stiff dough. (If dough seems dry, add 1 to 2 more tablespoons cold water.) Turn the dough out onto your work surface and knead for a minute or two, then divide the dough into 12 balls about the size of a Ping-Pong ball. Place the dough balls on a plate and cover with plastic wrap. Refrigerate for about 30 minutes while you prepare the filling, so the dough can rest before rolling it out.

To make the filling, remove and discard the stems of the tomatoes, then finely dice them. Set aside in a bowl. Heat the canola oil over medium heat in a heavy-bottomed skillet and add the onion and garlic. Sauté for 3 to 4 minutes until the onion is translucent, then stir in the tomatoes, pepper, cinnamon, cloves, raisins, and olives. Continue to sauté for about 7 minutes, stirring occasionally, until most of the liquid has evaporated.

Meanwhile, peel the plantain and cut it crosswise into ½-inch slices. Cut each slice into quarters. Melt the butter in a separate small skillet over medium heat and add the plantain. Sauté for 4 to 6 minutes, turning the plantain pieces to brown all sides. When the tomatoes are ready, add the plantain and stir to combine. Remove from the heat and set aside.

(continued)

Preheat the oven to 350 degrees F. Remove the dough from the refrigerator. Lightly flour a work surface and roll each piece of dough into a circle about 3 inches in diameter. Place about 1 tablespoon of the filling on one half of the circle, leaving a ½-inch border free of filling. Moisten the edge with water and fold the dough in half over the filling. Press the edges together and score with a fork to seal. Place on a dry baking sheet and bake for 15 to 20 minutes, until lightly browned. Serve immediately, with remaining filling on the side. Pass Lowfat Crema (page 34) as a condiment, if desired.

Each empanada provides:

143	Calories	23 g	Carbohydrate
2 g	Protein	298 mg	Sodium
5 g	Fat	9 mg	Cholesterol
1 g	Dietary Fiber		

Mango, Jicama, and Feta Quesadillas

ALMOST INSTANT

These light and delicious quesadillas make a festive summer supper.
Be sure to use a perfectly ripe mango. Ripe mangoes have a mostly
yellow skin with some reddish spots but very little green. They yield
to slight pressure but are not mushy. If you can find only green
mangoes at the market, bring one home and allow it to sit at room
temperature for a few days until ripe.

Yield: 6 appetizer servings

Fresh serrano chile	1	**small**
Cumin seeds	**1½**	**teaspoons**
Jicama, peeled and finely diced	1	**cup (about ⅓ pound)**
Fresh cilantro leaves, minced	**¼**	**cup**
Fresh-squeezed lime juice	2	**tablespoons**
Pure chile powder	1	**teaspoon**
Salt		**A pinch**
Black pepper		**A few grinds**
Fresh mango	1	**medium (¾ pound)**
Flour tortillas*	3	**standard-size**
Mild feta cheese crumbled	2	**ounces, (½ cup)**

(continued)

---

*Some brands of flour tortillas are made with lard. Read the labels and select a lard-free variety.

Remove and discard the stem of the chile and scrape out the seeds and membrane for a milder dish. Finely mince the chile and set it aside in a bowl. In a dry skillet over medium heat, toast the cumin seeds, stirring frequently, until they begin to brown and emit a toasted aroma. Transfer the seeds to a mortar and pestle or spice grinder, and coarsely grind them. Add the cumin to the bowl, along with the jicama, cilantro, lime juice, chile powder, salt, and pepper. Stir to combine well and set aside.

Using a sharp knife, slice all the way through the mango alongside the pit on both broad sides of the fruit. Place one bowl-shaped half of the mango cut side up on the work surface and slice the fruit to, but not through, the skin in one direction and then the other to create a checkerboard pattern. Turn the skin inside out to expose the diced mango and cut the chunks from the skin. Repeat this process with the other half of the mango. Cut the remaining fruit from the pit, peel and dice it, and set it aside. (Alternatively, use a sharp paring knife to peel the mango, then slice the fruit from the pit. Cut the mango fruit into small dice and set aside.)

Heat a cast-iron skillet or griddle over medium-high heat until it is hot enough to sizzle a drop of water. Place 1 tortilla in the pan and allow it to heat up for about 1 minute. Turn the tortilla over and arrange a third of the cheese evenly over half of the tortilla. Top the cheese evenly with a third of the mango. Cook for about 3 minutes, turning once or twice, until the tortilla has begun to brown but is not completely crisp.

Use a spatula to transfer the quesadilla to a plate, distribute a third of the jicama mixture evenly over the mango and cheese, and fold the tortilla over to cover the filling. Repeat this procedure for the remaining 2 quesadillas. (If you have more than one cast-iron skillet, you can cook more than 1 quesadilla at a time.)

Slice each quesadilla into 4 wedges and arrange the wedges in a single layer on a colorful serving platter. Garnish with cilantro sprigs, if you wish. Serve hot or at room temperature.

━━━━━━━━━━━━━━━━━━

Each serving provides:

162	Calories	28 g	Carbohydrate
4 g	Protein	167 mg	Sodium
4 g	Fat	8 mg	Cholesterol
2 g	Dietary Fiber		

Nopalito and Tomato Quesadillas

When they are cut, raw prickly pear cactus paddles, or nopales, have a slimy quality similar to that of okra. This cooks away, however, to yield a flavor that is a cross between limes and green beans. This is a light but satisfying first course.

Yield: 12 appetizer servings

Fresh nopales	$\frac{1}{2}$	**pound**
Fresh pear tomatoes	$\frac{1}{2}$	**pound**
Fresh poblano chile	1	**large (about $\frac{1}{4}$ pound)**
Cumin seeds	1	**teaspoon**
Canola oil	1	**tablespoon**
Green onions	2	**medium, minced**
Garlic	1	**clove, minced**
Salt	$\frac{1}{2}$	**teaspoon**
Flour tortillas*	8	**standard-size**
Part-skim queso fresco, crumbled	4	**ounces (1 cup)**

The thorns of the nopales, which are lodged under the small bumps that irregularly dot the paddles, usually have been shaved off by the grower. If not, use the dull edge of a knife blade to scrape off the thorns, taking care not to stick yourself. Do not remove the peel, however. Lay the nopales flat on your work surface and cut off and discard $\frac{1}{4}$-inch of the outer rim and the base end. Slice the paddles lengthwise into $\frac{1}{4}$-inch strips,

*Some brands of flour tortillas are made with lard. Read the labels and select a lard-free variety.

then cut the strips into 1-inch pieces. Place the cactus strips in a saucepan and cover with water. Bring to a boil, reduce the heat to medium-high, cover the pan, and cook for about 15 minutes, until fork-tender. (The cooking time may vary depending on the freshness of the cactus.) Drain into a colander and rinse well with cold water. Pat dry with a tea towel and set aside.

Meanwhile, chop the tomatoes and place them in a bowl. Remove and discard the stem, seeds, and membrane from the chile. Finely dice it and add to the bowl. Add the cooked cactus and toss to combine.

Crush the cumin seeds with a mortar and pestle. Heat the 1 tablespoon oil over medium heat in a heavy-bottomed skillet. Stir in the cumin seeds, green onions, and garlic and sauté for 1 to 2 minutes. Add the tomato mixture and salt. Increase the heat to medium-high and cook, stirring occasionally, for about 10 minutes, until all of the liquid has evaporated.

Heat for a moment over medium-high heat. Lay a tortilla in the skillet. Place a quarter of the tomato mixture on top. Sprinkle with a quarter of the cheese and place another tortilla on top. Cook until golden brown, about 3 minutes. Flip the quesadilla and continue to cook for 2 to 3 minutes to brown the other side. Keep warm in the oven while you cook the remaining quesadillas using the remaining oil as needed. Cut each quesadilla into 6 wedges. Serve immediately.

Each serving provides:

74	Calories	21 g	Carbohydrate
6 g	Protein	285 mg	Sodium
7 g	Fat	8 mg	Cholesterol
2 g	Dietary Fiber		

Mushroom and Cheese Quesadillas

ALMOST INSTANT

This wonderful mushroom mixture could be used for tostadas, tacos, or enchiladas, but we think it's especially well suited to quick-cooking quesadillas. They make a delicious appetizer when cut into wedges, but they can also be served as an entrée for four, 1 whole quesadilla per diner. Serve with a selection of table salsas.

Yield: 6 appetizer servings

Fresh serrano chile	1	medium
Cumin seeds	½	teaspoon
Button mushrooms	½	pound
White onion	½	medium, sliced
Salt	¼	teaspoon
Mexican Vegetable Stock*	½	cup
Dry sherry	1	tablespoon
Flour tortillas**	4	standard-size
Mild cheddar cheese, shredded	3	ounces (¾ cup)

Remove and discard the stems of the chile and scrape out the seeds and membrane for a milder dish. Finely mince the chile and set aside. Crush the cumin seeds with a mortar and pestle. Set aside. Brush or wipe any loose dirt particles from the mushrooms and thinly slice them.

*If you do not have Mexican Vegetable Stock on hand, make a batch according to the directions on page 38, or dissolve 1 large low-sodium vegetable broth cube in 3 cups hot water.

**Some brands of flour tortillas are made with lard. Read the labels and select a lard-free variety.

Place the mushrooms, onion, chile, and cumin seeds in a skillet or sauté pan that has a tight-fitting lid. Sprinkle with the salt and pour in the stock. Cover the pan and cook over medium heat 10 minutes. Remove the lid and continue to stir and cook if more than a tablespoon or so of liquid remains in the pan. When the mixture is fairly dry, turn off the heat and stir in the sherry. Set aside.

Heat a cast-iron griddle or heavy-bottomed skillet over medium heat for a few minutes. Place 1 of the tortillas in the pan and cook for about a minute. Turn the tortilla over and distribute a quarter of the cheese over half of the tortilla. Top the cheese with a quarter of the mushroom mixture. Use a spatula to fold the tortilla in half, enclosing the filling. Cook, turning once or twice, until the cheese begins to melt and the tortilla is browning, but do not let the tortilla get too crisp. If the tortilla is browning too quickly, reduce the heat a bit.

Repeat the process with the remaining 2 tortillas until all the quesadillas are cooked. Cut each quesadilla into 4 wedges and serve warm or at room temperature.

Each serving provides:

124	Calories	13 g	Carbohydrate
6 g	Protein	216 mg	Sodium
6 g	Fat	13 mg	Cholesterol
1 g	Dietary Fiber		

Black Bean Patties with Tomatillo Sauce

ALMOST INSTANT

This is a simple and economical do-ahead appetizer. The cooked beans are combined with seasonings and ground pumpkin seeds to create delicious patties that require no further cooking. If you serve these with corn chips, any leftover sauce will be devoured as a dip by your guests.

Yield: 6 appetizer servings

The sauce

Fresh tomatillos	$^3/_4$	pound (9 medium)
Salt	$^1/_4$	teaspoon
Pure chile powder	$^1/_2$	teaspoon
Ground cumin	$^1/_4$	teaspoon
Lowfat Crema (page 34)	2	tablespoons
Arrowroot powder	2	tablespoons

The patties

Cooked black beans*	2	cups, drained
Raw unsalted pumpkin seeds	$^1/_4$	cup
Canned diced mild green chiles	3	tablespoons
Granulated garlic	$^1/_4$	teaspoon

To make the sauce, remove and discard the husks of the tomatillos, rinse them, and place in a saucepan with the salt. Cover with water and bring to a boil. Reduce the heat and simmer

---

*Cook dried beans according to the directions on page 31, or use canned beans that do not contain additives.

about 10 minutes, until the tomatillos are tender. Drain and place them in a food processor along with the chile powder and cumin. Pulse to combine. Add the crema and arrowroot powder, then purée until smooth. Transfer to a small pan and cook over medium heat 2 to 3 minutes, until mixture thickens. Do not overcook, as it will get gummy. Set aside.

Meanwhile, place the beans in a bowl and mash them thoroughly to form a thick paste. Place the pumpkin seeds in a small food processor or blender and finely chop them to a coarse crumb consistency. Add them to the beans along with the chiles and garlic, stirring well to combine. (If the paste seems too dry, moisten with 1 to 2 tablespoons of water.)

Form the bean mixture into 3-inch patties and place them on a large platter. (If you are not going to serve the patties right away, cover the platter with plastic wrap so they do not dry out.) Transfer the tomatillo sauce to a serving bowl and allow guests to spoon the sauce over the patties.

Each serving provides:

145	Calories	21 g	Carbohydrate
8 g	Protein	188 mg	Sodium
4 g	Fat	2 mg	Cholesterol
3 g	Dietary Fiber		

Jalapeños Stuffed with Guacamole and Cucumber

ALMOST INSTANT, VEGAN

Canned pickled jalapeños range in intensity from moderately hot to incendiary, so beware these morsels if you can't take the heat! The cucumber lends a cooling counterpoint, as well as a nice crunch. We recommend serving a mild appetizer alongside this one, so guests who do not enjoy spicy food can have something else to eat, and those who do like spicy food can alternate between the two. Since bread helps to douse the fire of hot chiles, the Cheese Toasts with Green Chiles, Cilantro, and Garlic (page 84) is a good choice. Plan on 1 to 2 stuffed chiles per person. For an extra-pretty presentation, you may drizzle the stuffed peppers with crema and dust them with chile powder.

Yield: 12 stuffed chiles

Ripe Haas avocado	1	**medium (about ½ pound)**
Fresh-squeezed lime juice	1	**tablespoon**
Pure chile powder	2	**teaspoons**
Garlic	1	**clove, minced**
Salt		**A pinch**
Cucumber, diced	½	**cup (about ¼ pound)**
Red onion, minced	¼	**cup**
Pickled whole jalapeño chiles	12	**medium, drained**

Cut open the avocado and remove the pit (see page 6). With a spoon, scrape the avocado out of the skin into a bowl. Add the lime juice and mash the avocado with a fork. Add the chile powder, garlic, and salt and stir vigorously to create a fairly smooth texture.

Peel a cucumber and slice it in half lengthwise. With a spoon, scrape out and discard the seeds. Finely mince the cucumber to measure ½ cup. Gently stir the cucumber and onion into the avocado mixture until well combined.

Place a chile flat on your cutting board and, holding it by its stem, use a sharp knife to slit the upper side of the chile lengthwise, leaving the bottom side intact. With a spoon, gently scrape out and discard the seeds and membrane. Use a spoon to fill the chile generously with the avocado mixture. Repeat this process until you have filled all the chiles.

Place them on a small platter and serve immediately, or refrigerate for up to an hour before serving. The stuffed jalapeños are good cold or at room temperature.

━ ━ ━ ━ ━ ━ ━ ━ ━

Each chile provides:

51	Calories	3 g	Carbohydrate
1 g	Protein	70 mg	Sodium
5 g	Fat	0 mg	Cholesterol
1 g	Dietary Fiber		

Roasted Peanuts with Chile and Lime Juice

VEGAN

Nuts are always a welcome appetizer. These peanuts are crunchy, salty, and just a little spicy, which means they awaken the appetite gently. Serve them anytime, alone or as part of an antojito buffet.

Yield: 12 appetizer servings

Shelled raw unsalted peanuts	2	**cups**
Fresh-squeezed lime juice	1	**tablespoon**
Pure chile powder	1	**teaspoon**
Salt	¼	**teaspoon**

Preheat the oven to 400 degrees F. Bring 4 cups of water to a boil in a small saucepan. Drop the peanuts into the water and boil them for 2 minutes. Transfer to a colander and rinse with cold water. Drain the peanuts well. Remove and discard the skins. Spread the peanuts out on a dry baking sheet.

Place the peanuts in the oven and roast for 15 to 20 minutes, until lightly browned, shaking or stirring the nuts once midway through the cooking time so they roast evenly. Transfer the hot peanuts to a bowl and toss with the lime juice, then with the chile powder and salt. Serve warm or at room temperature.

Each serving provides:

143	Calories	4 g	Carbohydrate
7 g	Protein	51 mg	Sodium
12 g	Fat	0 mg	Cholesterol
2 g	Dietary Fiber		

Spicy Toasted Pumpkin Seeds

ALMOST INSTANT, VEGAN

Pumpkin seeds are popular as an ingredient in Mexican cooking, but here they make a finger-licking snack.

Yield: 12 appetizer servings

Olive oil	1	tablespoon
Ground cumin	½	teaspoon
Pure chile powder	½	teaspoon
Granulated garlic	¼	teaspoon
Raw unsalted pumpkin seeds	2	cups

Heat the oil in a large heavy-bottomed skillet over medium heat. Add the cumin, chile powder, and garlic. Heat through for about a minute, stirring to combine. Add the pumpkin seeds and stir to coat them with the spices. When the seeds begin to pop, stir or shake the pan constantly until they have all popped and turned golden brown, about 10 minutes. Serve warm or at room temperature. Any leftover seeds may be refrigerated for several weeks in an airtight container.

Each serving provides:

144	Calories	4 g	Carbohydrate
9 g	Protein	139 mg	Sodium
12 g	Fat	0 mg	Cholesterol
1 g	Dietary Fiber		

Pumpkin Seed Cheese Spread

ALMOST INSTANT

This spread can be made well in advance and will gently prepare your guests for the spicy dishes that may follow. Pumpkin seeds, when toasted, develop a nutty flavor that blends perfectly with the cheeses. Serve with slices of sweet baguette or with crisp crackers.

Yield: 8 appetizer servings

Raw unsalted pumpkin seeds	$\frac{1}{4}$	**cup**
Cumin seeds	$1\frac{1}{2}$	**teaspoons**
Part-skim ricotta cheese	$\frac{1}{3}$	**cup**
Mild feta cheese, crumbled	3	**ounces ($\frac{3}{4}$ cup)**
Garlic	2	**cloves, minced**
Fresh-squeezed lime juice	1	**tablespoon**
Dried thyme	$\frac{1}{4}$	**teaspoon**
Pure chile powder	$\frac{1}{4}$	**teaspoon**
Sweet baguette	1	**1-pound loaf**

Place the pumpkin seeds in a heavy-bottomed skillet over medium heat. Shake the pan or stir the seeds frequently as they heat for a few minutes. When the seeds begin to pop, add the cumin seeds to the pan and stir continuously as the pumpkin seeds finish roasting. When almost all the pumpkin seeds have popped and are lightly browned, transfer them directly to a food processor. Add the cheeses, garlic, lime juice, and thyme and purée until fairly smooth. Transfer to a ramekin or serving bowl and dust with the chile powder. Serve immediately with ½-inch baguette slices, or refrigerate for several hours so the flavor can develop. Return the spread to room temperature before serving.

Each serving provides:

233	Calories	31 g	Carbohydrate
9 g	Protein	489 mg	Sodium
7 g	Fat	13 mg	Cholesterol
2 g	Dietary Fiber		

Guacamole

ALMOST INSTANT, VEGAN

Guacamole is one of the national dishes of Mexico. It is best prepared just before serving, but you may hold it over for an hour or so, if necessary, in a tightly closed container in the refrigerator. We prefer to mash the avocado coarsely, rather than whipping it, for a more authentic texture. If you have garden-fresh pear tomatoes, you may substitute them for the canned ones. Traditionally, of course, guacamole is served with crisp tortilla chips, but it also is delicious as a dip for jicama, celery, and red bell pepper strips.

Yield: 2 cups

Fresh serrano chile	1	**medium**
Ripe Haas avocados	2	**medium (1 pound)**
Fresh-squeezed lime juice	1½	**tablespoons**
White onion, minced	⅓	**cup**
Garlic	1	**clove, minced**
Salt	¼	**teaspoon plus ⅛ teaspoon**
Black pepper		**A few grinds**
Canned whole pear tomatoes	2,	**drained and minced**
Fresh cilantro leaves, minced	¼	**cup**

Remove and discard the stem of the chile and scrape out the seeds and membrane for a milder dish. Finely mince the chile and set aside in a bowl. Cut open the avocados and remove the pits (see page 6). With a spoon, scrape the avocado flesh out of the skin into the bowl. Add the lime juice, onion, garlic, chile, salt, and pepper and mash with a fork until no large chunks remain; you do not want a whipped texture. Stir in the tomatoes and cilantro and serve.

Each ¼-cup serving provides:

81	Calories	5 g	Carbohydrate
1 g	Protein	118 mg	Sodium
7 g	Fat	0 mg	Cholesterol
1 g	Dietary Fiber		

Nachos with Beans and Pickled Jalapeños

ALMOST INSTANT

Although they are not traditional Mexican cuisine, nachos are a favorite finger food north of the border. This version has plenty of beans and gets some zing from pickled jalapeños.

Yield: 6 appetizer servings

Fresh pear tomatoes	½	**pound**
Fresh parsley leaves, minced	¼	**cup**
Ground cumin	½	**teaspoon**
Pure chile powder	½	**teaspoon**
Salt	½	**teaspoon**
Fresh-squeezed lemon juice	2	**tablespoons**
Cooked pinto beans*	1½	**cups, drained**
Bean cooking or canning liquid	3	**tablespoons**
Lightly salted tortilla strips	8	**ounces**
Jack cheese, shredded	4	**ounces (1 cup)**
Pickled sliced jalapeño chiles	¼	**cup, drained**

Remove and discard the stem end of the tomatoes, then dice them. Place the tomatoes in a bowl and toss with the parsley. Combine the cumin, chile powder, and salt then sprinkle it over the tomatoes. Add the lemon juice, toss to combine, and set aside.

*Cook dried beans according to the instructions on page 31, or purchase canned beans that do not contain additives.

Preheat the oven to 350 degrees F. Place the beans in a food processor with the bean cooking liquid and purée until smooth. Mound ½ of the tortilla strips on the bottom of a large, ovenproof serving dish and top evenly with the beans and cheese. Place in the oven and bake for about 8 minutes, until the cheese melts. Remove from the oven and top with the tomato mixture and chiles, or serve the chiles on the side. Serve immediately with the remaining strips on the side.

Each serving provides:

383	Calories	49 g	Carbohydrate
15 g	Protein	557 mg	Sodium
15 g	Fat	13 mg	Cholesterol
7 g	Dietary Fiber		

Tortillas with Cheese, Poblano Chiles, Cinnamon, and Cumin

ALMOST INSTANT

Queso fundido, *as it is called in Mexico, is a wonderful array of melted cheese that is scooped up with flour tortillas. The delicious mix of spices in this recipe will leave you scraping the pan!*

Yield: 8 appetizer servings

Fresh poblano chiles	2	**large (about ½ pound)**
Flour tortillas*	8	**standard-size**
Gold tequila	1	**tablespoon**
Ground cinnamon	¼	**teaspoon**
Ground cumin	¼	**teaspoon**
Jack cheese, shredded	8	**ounces (2 cups)**

Roast the chiles on a hot grill or under the broiler for about 5 minutes, or until the skin is uniformly charred. Turn and blacken the other side. Place them in a paper or plastic bag, close the bag, and set aside at room temperature; the steam inside the bag will finish cooking the chiles. When they are cool enough to handle, remove and discard the skin, stem, and seeds. Cut the chiles lengthwise into thin strips. (You may do this in advance and refrigerate the cleaned chiles until needed.)

*Some brands of flour tortillas are made with lard. Read the labels and select a lard-free variety.

Meanwhile, wrap the tortillas in foil and place them in a warm oven. Put the tequila in a small skillet over medium heat and add the cinnamon, cumin, and chiles. Cook for several minutes to burn off the tequila. Transfer the chile mixture to a small plate. Return the skillet to medium-low heat and add half of the cheese, then sprinkle the chile mixture over it. Top with the remaining half of the cheese. The cheese will slowly melt and just begin to bubble. Transfer the skillet to the table and serve immediately with the warm tortillas.

Each serving provides:

214	Calories	20 g	Carbohydrate
10 g	Protein	207 mg	Sodium
11 g	Fat	25 mg	Cholesterol
1 g	Dietary Fiber		

Black Bean Purée with Fresh Guacamole

ALMOST INSTANT, VEGAN

For a visual treat, present this delicious dip in a bright red or yellow shallow bowl, with a few sprigs of cilantro, minced onion, and/or a dusting of red chile powder for garnish. Serve with tortilla chips and/or raw jicama and bell pepper strips.

Yield: 8 appetizer servings

Fresh serrano chile	1	medium
Cooked black beans*	2	cups, drained
Tomato juice	2	tablespoons
Fresh-squeezed lime juice	2	tablespoons
Garlic	1	small clove, chopped
Dried Mexican oregano	1	teaspoon
Salt	¼	teaspoon plus a pinch
Ripe Haas avocado	1	medium (about ½ pound)
White onion, grated	2	tablespoons
Fresh cilantro leaves, minced	2	tablespoons
Fresh-squeezed lemon juice	1	teaspoon
Black pepper		Several grinds

Remove the stem of the chile, cut it in half lengthwise, and scrape out the seeds, if a milder dish is desired. Coarsely chop the chile.

*Cook dried beans according to the instructions on page 31, or purchase canned beans that do not contain additives.

In a food processor, combine the chile, beans, tomato juice, lime juice, garlic, oregano, and the ¼ teaspoon salt. Purée to a fairly smooth consistency. (At this point, the purée can be refrigerated in a covered container for up to a few days.)

Just before serving, place the purée in a pretty, shallow serving bowl, smoothing out the top with a rubber spatula.

Cut open the avocado and remove the pit (see page 6). With a spoon, scrape the avocado out of the skin into a bowl. Coarsely mash the avocado with the onion, cilantro, lemon juice, the pinch salt, and black pepper until no large chunks remain. Do not overmix; you do not want a whipped texture. Spread the mixture over the black beans, leaving a 1-inch border of beans free of the avocado purée. Garnish as described in the recipe introduction, if desired, and serve immediately.

Each serving provides:

97	Calories	13 g	Carbohydrate
5 g	Protein	88 mg	Sodium
4 g	Fat	0 mg	Cholesterol
2 g	Dietary Fiber		

Jicama and Roasted Red Bell Pepper Plate

ALMOST INSTANT, VEGAN

This refreshing appetizer is delightful in its simplicity. It can be made ahead of time and refrigerated until serving time. One of the wonderful qualities of jicama is that it retains its crispness for days—even after it is cut.

Yield: 8 appetizer servings

Red bell pepper	1	**large**
Jicama	1	**pound**
Fresh-squeezed lime juice	2	**tablespoons**
Pure chile powder	1	**teaspoon**
Salt	1/8	**teaspoon**

Roast the bell pepper under a hot broiler, on a grill, or over an open flame on the stovetop. Turn it frequently until the skin is uniformly charred black. Transfer the charred pepper to a plastic or paper bag, close the bag, and set aside for about 15 minutes. When the pepper is cool enough to handle, peel off the charred skin and discard the seeds, stem, and white membrane. Dice the pepper flesh finely and set aside.

Meanwhile, peel the jicama and cut it in half from stem to root. Lay each piece cut side down on the work surface and cut into 1/4-inch slices. Toss these slices in a bowl with the lime juice, then make a ring of overlapping slices around the outside of a colorful serving plate, retaining the lime juice. Mound the diced bell pepper in the center of the ring. Drizzle the lime juice evenly over the jicama and bell pepper, then dust the jicama with the chile powder and salt.

Serve immediately or cover with plastic wrap and refrigerate for up to 2 days. Place a small fork on the plate before serving. Diners use the fork to place a small mound of bell pepper on a jicama slice before eating it with their fingers.

Each serving provides:

25	Calories	6 g	Carbohydrate
1 g	Protein	39 mg	Sodium
0 g	Fat	0 mg	Cholesterol
1 g	Dietary Fiber		

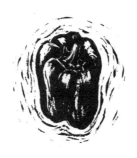

Cornbread with Whole Kernels

As far as we know, cornbread is not a traditional Mexican food, but it goes so well with Mexican soups, beans, and egg dishes that we couldn't resist including our favorite simple cornbread recipe. Of course, it's also a wonderful appetizer.

Yield: 8 appetizer servings

Canola oil	1	tablespoon plus ¼ teaspoon
Cultured lowfat buttermilk	1	cup
Egg	1	large
Honey	2	tablespoons
Coarse yellow cornmeal	¾	cup
Unbleached flour	¾	cup
Baking powder	2	teaspoons
Pure chile powder	2	teaspoons
Salt	¼	teaspoon
Corn kernels, fresh or frozen*	1	cup

Preheat the oven to 375 degrees F. Use the ¼ teaspoon oil to rub a square 8-inch baking dish. Set the oiled dish aside.

In a medium mixing bowl, stir together the 1 tablespoon oil, the buttermilk, egg, and honey until well blended and smooth. In a separate small mixing bowl, stir together the cornmeal, flour, baking powder, chile powder, and salt until well combined. Pour the dry ingredients into the buttermilk mixture and beat vigorously for about 1 minute, until the batter is smooth and homogenous.

*If you are using fresh corn, you will need about 2 medium ears to yield 1 cup kernels.

If using frozen corn, rinse it with hot water for a moment or two to melt the ice crystals and drain thoroughly. Stir the corn kernels into the batter until well distributed, then pour the batter into the oiled dish and bake for 30 to 35 minutes, until a toothpick inserted in its center comes out clean. Remove the cornbread from the oven and allow it to stand at room temperature for at least 5 minutes before cutting it into sixteen 2 × 2-inch squares. Serve hot or at room temperature, with butter or another spread, if you wish.

Each serving provides:

167	Calories	30 g	Carbohydrate
5 g	Protein	201 mg	Sodium
4 g	Fat	29 mg	Cholesterol
2 g	Dietary Fiber		

Cheese Toasts with Green Chiles, Cilantro, and Garlic

ALMOST INSTANT

These delicious little toasts get their Mexican character from the combination of mild green chiles and cilantro. They combine wonderfully on an appetizer buffet table with spicier dishes, such as the Jalapeños Stuffed with Guacamole and Cucumber (page 82).

Yield: 6 appetizer servings

Mild feta cheese, crumbled	2	ounces (½ cup)
Mozzarella cheese, shredded	2	ounces (½ cup)
Canned diced mild green chiles	⅓	cup
Fresh cilantro leaves, minced	2	tablespoons
Garlic	1	clove, minced
Baguette	18	½-inch slices

Preheat the broiler. In a bowl, combine the cheeses with the chiles, cilantro, and garlic. Toss until well combined. Place the baguette slices on a dry baking sheet and broil them until lightly toasted on one side. Remove the baking sheet from the oven, turn the bread slices over, and place a heaping mound of the cheese mixture on each slice. Return to the broiler for 2 to 3 minutes, until the cheese melts and the bread browns a little around the edges. Serve hot.

Each serving provides:

201	Calories	28 g	Carbohydrate
8 g	Protein	559 mg	Sodium
5 g	Fat	14 mg	Cholesterol
1 g	Dietary Fiber		

Salads and Cold Vegetable Dishes

The traditional Mexican meal does not include a salad as we know it, but includes raw vegetables to be used as condiments with dishes such as tacos, tostadas, and tamales. On balance, the average person in Mexico probably eats a fair amount of "salad" in this manner.

Since we enjoy a refreshing leafy salad with almost every meal, we've included three such dishes in this chapter that are designed to combine well with the flavors of Mexican main courses. In addition, we have invented a number of hearty raw and cooked vegetable dishes that may be served cold or at room temperature, dressed with a sauce. This type of *ensalada* can be considered authentically Mexican.

This chapter is intended to broaden your definition of salads and to introduce you to some of the unusual ingredients and seasonings of Mexico.

Tips and Tools

- Excellent salads depend on fresh, crisp, flavorful produce. Cooks in Mexico shop the market almost daily for the best quality fruits and vegetables—do the same, if your schedule permits.

- Take the time to wash salad greens carefully, since dirt and sand are frequently lodged among the leaves. Be sure to dry the leaves, so water clinging to them doesn't dilute the dressing.

- Large bowls and tongs or salad utensils are essential for mixing and serving salads. You may serve individual salads on plates or in bowls, as you wish.

- A whisk makes quick work of dressings. We also depend on a manual juicer or a lemon reamer for extracting citrus juices.

Carrot Salad with Cilantro and Lemon

ALMOST INSTANT, VEGAN

*The splash of lemon juice is a nice counterpoint to the sweetness
of the carrot. Cilantro lends its unique flavor, but does not overpower
the salad.*

Yield: 2 servings

Carrot	1 **large**
Green onions	2 **medium, minced**
Fresh cilantro leaves, minced	2 **tablespoons**
Fresh-squeezed lemon juice	1 **tablespoon**
Cayenne	**A pinch**

Scrub the carrot clean and grate it. Place the grated carrot in a
bowl along with the green onions, cilantro, and lemon juice. Toss
to combine. Sprinkle with the cayenne and chill for about
15 minutes before serving.

Each serving provides:

24	Calories	6 g	Carbohydrate
1 g	Protein	18 mg	Sodium
0 g	Fat	0 mg	Cholesterol
2 g	Dietary Fiber		

Cherry Tomato Salad with Green Onions and Cilantro

ALMOST INSTANT, VEGAN

The colors and flavors combined in this recipe are lively, bright, and satisfying. It is a wonderful, simple salad appropriate to serve with any Mexican or Southwest-inspired entrée.

Yield: 6 side-dish servings

Cherry tomatoes	1	**pound (16 large)**
Green onions	6	**medium, minced**
Garlic	1	**clove, minced**
Pure chile powder	2	**teaspoons**
Dried Mexican oregano	2	**teaspoons**
Salt	⅛	**teaspoon**
Black pepper		**Several grinds**
Fresh-squeezed lime juice	2	**tablespoons**
Apple cider vinegar	2	**tablespoons**
Fresh cilantro leaves, minced	¼	**cup**
Butter lettuce	1	**medium head**

Wash the tomatoes and pat them dry. Halve the tomatoes and toss them in a bowl with the green onions, garlic, chile powder, oregano, salt, and pepper. Add the lime juice, vinegar, and cilantro and toss again. Allow to marinate for up to a few hours at room temperature.

Just before serving, wash and dry the lettuce leaves and tear them into bite-size pieces. Combine them with the tomato mixture and serve.

Each serving provides:

33	Calories	7 g	Carbohydrate
2 g	Protein	66 mg	Sodium
1 g	Fat	0 mg	Cholesterol
2 g	Dietary Fiber		

Jicama and Cucumber Salad with Orange Lime Marinade

Jicama is a woody-looking root vegetable with a crunchy texture and a sweet flavor. This salad makes a delicious palate-cleanser for a spicy main dish such as Stuffed Chiles with Savory Cocoa Mole (page 248).

Yield: 8 side-dish servings

Jicama	1	pound
Fresh-squeezed orange juice	½	cup
Fresh-squeezed lime juice	2	tablespoons
Ground coriander	¼	teaspoon
Pure chile powder	½	teaspoon
Salt	¼	teaspoon
Cucumber	1	medium
Fresh cilantro leaves, minced	3	tablespoons

Cut the jicama in half from stem to tip, then cut each piece in half lengthwise. Peel the jicama quarters, discard the peel, and cut the jicama into matchsticks. Place in a large glass or ceramic bowl.

Whisk together the orange juice, lime juice, coriander, chile powder, and salt. Pour over the jicama and toss to coat. Let stand at room temperature for about 1 hour.

Peel the cucumber and slice it in half lengthwise. Use a spoon to scoop out the seeds and discard them. Cut each piece in half lengthwise, then cut the strips crosswise into ¼-inch pieces. Add the cucumber to the jicama, along with the cilantro. Toss and serve.

Each serving provides:

32	Calories	7 g	Carbohydrate
1 g	Protein	72 mg	Sodium
0 g	Fat	0 mg	Cholesterol
1 g	Dietary Fiber		

Cauliflower Corn Salad with Orange Dressing

VEGAN

The colors of this salad are bright and beautiful. We like the crunch of fresh uncooked corn, but thawed frozen corn may be used. This salad combines very well with other dishes, but will also carry a light summertime luncheon, served with flour tortillas and Salsa Fresca (page 56).

Yield: 8 side-dish servings

Fresh cauliflower, diced	**4**	**cups (1 pound)**
Corn kernels, fresh or frozen*	**1½**	**cups**
Cherry tomatoes	**½**	**pound, halved (8 large)**
Green onions	**3**	**medium, minced**
Fresh cilantro leaves, minced	**⅓**	**cup**
Canola oil	**2**	**tablespoons**
Fresh-squeezed orange juice	**⅓**	**cup**
Fresh-squeezed lemon juice	**1**	**tablespoon**
Ground cumin	**1**	**teaspoon**
Pure chile powder	**¼**	**teaspoon**
Salt	**¼**	**teaspoon**

Steam the cauliflower for 5 minutes, then rinse under cold water to stop the cooking. Drain well in a colander. In a large bowl, combine the cauliflower with the corn, tomatoes, green onions, and cilantro. Toss gently until well combined.

*If you are using fresh corn, you will need about 3 medium ears to yield 1½ cups kernels.

Put the oil in a medium bowl and whisk in the orange juice, lemon juice, cumin, chile powder, and salt. Pour over the vegetables and toss well. Allow the salad to marinate in the refrigerator 2 to 4 hours, or up to overnight, so the flavors can blend.

Each serving provides:

91	Calories	13 g	Carbohydrate
3 g	Protein	87 mg	Sodium
4 g	Fat	0 mg	Cholesterol
3 g	Dietary Fiber		

Nopalito Salad with Pickled Jalapeños

ALMOST INSTANT

Look for nopales (prickly pear cactus paddles) year-round in a well-stocked supermarket, or a Mexican specialty store. When cooked, they taste a little like tart green beans. Pickled jalapeño chiles are readily available, sold in glass jars. You may remove the seeds of the chiles as you mince them for a less spicy salad.

Yield: 6 side-dish servings

Fresh nopales	¾	**pound**
Fresh parsley leaves, minced	½	**cup**
Red onion, minced	¼	**cup**
Pickled jalapeño chile, minced	1	**tablespoon**
Olive oil	2	**tablespoons**
Fresh-squeezed lime juice	1	**tablespoon**
Butter lettuce leaves	6	**large**
Fresh tomato	1	**large, sliced**
Part-skim queso fresco, crumbled	2	**ounces (½ cup)**

The thorns of the nopales, which are lodged under the small bumps that irregularly dot the paddles, usually have been shaved off by the grower. If not, use the dull edge of a knife blade to scrape off the thorns of the cactus, taking care not to stick yourself. Do not remove the peel, however. Lay the paddles flat on your work surface and cut off and discard ¼-inch of the outer rim and the base end. Slice the paddles lengthwise into ¼-inch strips, then cut the strips into 1-inch pieces. Place the strips in a saucepan and cover with water. Bring to a boil, reduce the heat to medium-high, cover the pan, and cook for about 15 minutes, until fork-tender. (The cooking time may vary depending on the freshness of the cactus.) Drain into a colander and rinse well with cold water. Pat dry with a tea towel and set aside.

Place cooked cactus in a glass or ceramic bowl and add the parsley, onion, chile, olive oil, and lime juice. Toss to combine. Place a lettuce leaf on each individual serving plate and top each with an equal amount of the cactus. Arrange the tomato slices around the edge of each plate. Sprinkle with equal amounts of the cheese and serve.

Each serving provides:

82	Calories	4 g	Carbohydrate
3 g	Protein	90 mg	Sodium
7 g	Fat	5 mg	Cholesterol
1 g	Dietary Fiber		

Zucchini and Mushrooms in Spicy Lime Marinade

ALMOST INSTANT, VEGAN

This is a wonderful make-ahead dish for a potluck or picnic, since its flavor will continue to develop at room temperature for several hours. It can even be made a day ahead of time, though the mushrooms will lose some of their firmness. We enjoy this simple salad often in summer, when zucchini is abundant and cool vegetables are most appetizing.

Yield: 6 side-dish servings

Zucchini	3	**medium (1 pound)**
Button mushrooms	¾	**pound**
Cumin seeds	1	**teaspoon**
White onion	½	**medium, diced**
Olive oil	2	**tablespoons**
Pure chile powder	2	**teaspoons**
Garlic	2	**cloves, minced**
Salt	½	**teaspoon**
Black pepper		**A few grinds**
Fresh-squeezed lime juice	¼	**cup**
Fresh cilantro leaves, minced	¼	**cup**

Trim off and discard the ends of the zucchini. Slice each zucchini in half lengthwise, then cut the halves crosswise into ½-inch slices. Place the zucchini slices on a steamer rack over 2 inches of boiling water. Cover and steam 6 to 8 minutes, until barely fork-tender. Rinse with cold water and drain well.

Meanwhile, wipe the mushrooms clean and cut them in half from stem to cap, or in quarters if they are large. Crush the cumin seeds thoroughly with a mortar and pestle. Combine the zucchini and mushrooms in a bowl with the onion and olive oil. Toss to distribute the oil, then add the cumin seed, chile powder, garlic, salt, and pepper. Toss again. Add the lime juice and cilantro and toss until well combined.

Serve immediately or set aside at room temperature for up to several hours, stirring occasionally. Refrigerate the salad if you will be holding it overnight, but return it to room temperature before serving.

Each serving provides:

81	Calories	9 g	Carbohydrate
2 g	Protein	199 mg	Sodium
5 g	Fat	0 mg	Cholesterol
2 g	Dietary Fiber		

Fava and Black Beans with Jicama and Chipotle Chile Mayonnaise

Fresh fava beans are one of springtime's fleeting treasures. We buy them frequently during their brief season to enjoy in many different hot and cold dishes. This salad combines them with jicama, another underappreciated vegetable, for a slightly spicy feast of freshness.

Yield: 6 side-dish servings

Fresh fava beans, in pods	2	pounds (2½ cups shelled)
Fresh jicama, peeled and diced	1	cup (about ⅓ pound)
Cooked black beans*	1	cup, drained
Red onion, thinly sliced	½	cup
Chipotle Chile Mayonnaise (page 35)	3	tablespoons
Fresh-squeezed lime juice	2	tablespoons
Fresh cilantro leaves, minced	2	tablespoons
Granulated sugar	1	teaspoon
Ground cumin	¼	teaspoon
Butter lettuce leaves	4	cups

Bring 4 cups of water to a boil in a small saucepan. Shell the fava beans, discarding the pods, and add them to the boiling water. Return to a boil and cook only 2 minutes, then transfer to a

---

*Cook dried beans according to the instructions on page 31, or purchase canned beans that do not contain additives.

colander and rinse well with cold water to stop the cooking. When the beans are cool enough to handle, pop them out of their skins. Discard the skins and place the beans in a serving bowl with the jicama, black beans, and onion.

In a small bowl, stir together the chipotle chile mayonnaise, lime juice, cilantro, sugar, and cumin. Pour over the fava bean mixture and toss gently to combine. Just before serving, wash and dry the lettuce leaves and tear them into bite-size pieces to measure 4 cups. Distribute the lettuce equally among 6 salad plates and top each serving with a portion of the fava bean mixture. Serve immediately.

Each serving provides:

180	Calories	22 g	Carbohydrate
12 g	Protein	105 mg	Sodium
6 g	Fat	4 mg	Cholesterol
2 g	Dietary Fiber		

Tortilla Chip Salad with Lime Shallot Dressing

This colorful salad is as delicious as it is beautiful. Children love to crumble up the tortilla chips, so invite them to help.

Yield: 6 side-dish servings

Raw unsalted pumpkin seeds	¼	**cup**
Olive oil	¼	**cup**
Fresh-squeezed lime juice	⅓	**cup**
Shallots	2	**minced**
Honey	1	**tablespoon**
Cooked pinto beans*	1	**cup**
Jicama, grated	2	**cups**
Corn kernels, fresh or frozen**	1	**cup**
Red cabbage, shredded	1	**cup**
Green lettuce leaves, torn	3	**cups**
Fresh cilantro leaves	½	**cup**
Crumbled corn tortilla chips	1	**cup**

Place the pumpkin seeds in a dry heavy-bottomed skillet in a single layer over medium heat. Toast the seeds until they pop and begin to brown. Immediately remove them from the pan and set aside.

*Cook dried beans according to the instructions on page 31, or purchase canned beans that do not contain additives.

**If you are using fresh corn, you will need about 2 medium ears to yield 1 cup kernels.

Stir together the olive oil, lime juice, shallots, and honey to form a thick dressing. Set aside at room temperature. In a large bowl, toss together the pinto beans, jicama, corn, and red cabbage. Wash and dry lettuce leaves and tear them into bite-size pieces to measure 3 cups. Add the lettuce and cilantro and toss to combine. Just before serving, add the tortilla chips, toss to combine, then pour on the dressing, tossing gently one final time. Top with the pumpkin seeds and serve immediately.

Each serving provides:

243	Calories	27 g	Carbohydrate
7 g	Protein	73 mg	Sodium
14 g	Fat	0 mg	Cholesterol
3 g	Dietary Fiber		

Pasta Salad with Grilled Vegetables and Roasted Garlic Dressing

This slightly spicy, slightly smoky pasta salad is a summertime favorite. The ingredients intermingle deliciously to create an unconventional Mexican-inspired dish.

Yield: 8 side-dish servings

Garlic	2	**medium bulbs**
Yellow onions	2	**medium (1 pound)**
Extra-virgin olive oil	¼	**cup**
Zucchini	3	**medium (1 pound)**
Eggplant	1	**medium (1 pound)**
Dried pasta spirals	12	**ounces**
Fresh-squeezed lime juice	6	**tablespoons**
Chipotle chiles en adobo, minced	2	**tablespoons**
Salt	½	**teaspoon**
Part-skim queso fresco, crumbled	6	**ounces (1½ cups)**

Preheat a coal or gas grill to high. Without peeling, trim ¼-inch off the top end of the garlic bulbs to just expose the individual cloves. Wrap the whole bulbs in foil or place them in a ceramic garlic baker.

Trim off the ends of the onions and peel them. Cut the onions in half crosswise and lightly brush the cut sides with some of the olive oil. Place the onions on the grill, cut side down. Place the garlic on the grill. Cover the grill and bake 35 to

45 minutes, turning the onions every 8 to 10 minutes to cook evenly. The onions are done when they are soft and slightly charred. The garlic bulb is done when it is soft when gently squeezed. When done, remove the onion and garlic from the grill and set aside. Remove the garlic from the foil or garlic baker so it can cool.

Meanwhile, trim off and discard the ends of the zucchini and cut them in thirds lengthwise. Lightly brush the cut sides with some of the olive oil. Cut off and discard the stem end of the eggplant and cut it lengthwise into ½-inch slices. Brush the slices with just a bit of the olive oil. Place the zucchini and eggplant on the grill and cook about 15 to 20 minutes, turning several times during the cooking time. Allow them to char slightly and become fork-tender, but not mushy.

Meanwhile, bring several quarts of water to a boil in a large stockpot. Cook the pasta until al dente, and drain well. When done, preferably while the pasta is cooking, remove the zucchini and eggplant from the grill and allow them to cool slightly. Coarsely chop the onions, zucchini, and eggplant. Place the vegetables in a large bowl, add the drained pasta, and toss to combine.

Squeeze the roasted garlic paste into a blender. Add the lime juice, chile, and salt. Purée to combine. With the machine running, add the remaining olive oil. (You should have at least 3 tablespoons.) Pour over the vegetables and pasta, and toss to combine. Sprinkle on the queso fresco and toss again. Serve immediately, or refrigerate for several hours. Bring to room temperature before serving.

Each serving provides:

325	Calories	41 g	Carbohydrate
12 g	Protein	309 mg	Sodium
13 g	Fat	51 mg	Cholesterol
4 g	Dietary Fiber		

Leafy Greens with Cabbage and Mexicali Vinaigrette

ALMOST INSTANT, VEGAN

This simply scrumptious salad is a fine accompaniment to any of the main dishes in this book. It has been a "most-requested" recipe at our tastings.

Yield: 6 side-dish servings

Ripe Haas avocado	1	**medium (½ pound)**
Fresh-squeezed lime juice	2	**tablespoons**
Fresh cilantro leaves, minced	2	**tablespoons**
Apple cider vinegar	2	**tablespoons**
Honey	1	**teaspoon**
Ground cumin	½	**teaspoon**
Pure chile powder	½	**teaspoon**
Salt	¼	**teaspoon**
Black pepper		**A few grinds**
Mixed torn salad greens	4	**cups, loosely packed**
Green cabbage, shredded	1½	**cups, loosely packed**
Red onion, thinly sliced	¼	**cup**
Fresh tomato, chopped (or 2 canned pear tomatoes, chopped)	1	**medium**

Cut open the avocado and remove the pit (see page 6). Peel and dice the avocado and toss it in a small bowl with the lime juice, cilantro, vinegar, honey, cumin, chile powder, salt, and pepper. Set aside at room temperature while you put the salad together. (This much can be done up to a couple hours ahead of time.)

In a serving bowl, combine the greens, cabbage, onion, and tomato. Toss briefly, then add the avocado mixture, using a rubber spatula to scrape all of the dressing from the bowl. Toss the salad again and serve immediately.

Each serving provides:

70	Calories	7 g	Carbohydrate
2 g	Protein	103 mg	Sodium
5 g	Fat	0 mg	Cholesterol
2 g	Dietary Fiber		

Spinach Salad with Spiced Walnuts and Roasted Red Bell Pepper

VEGAN

This composed salad is fit for a fancy dinner, stunning in both visual appeal and flavor. If the walnuts and bell pepper are prepared several hours ahead of time, or the day before, the salad comes together in a snap.

Yield: 4 side-dish servings

Red bell pepper	1	small
Fresh spinach leaves, torn	6	cups
Raw walnuts, chopped	⅓	cup
Fresh-squeezed lime juice	2	teaspoons
Granulated garlic	¼	teaspoon
Pure chile powder	¼	teaspoon
Salt	¼	teaspoon
Fresh-squeezed orange juice	2	tablespoons
Apple cider vinegar	1	tablespoon
Olive oil	1	tablespoon
Red onion, thinly sliced	¼	cup
Black pepper		Several grinds
Fresh cilantro leaves, minced	2	tablespoons

Roast the bell pepper under a hot broiler, on a grill, or over an open flame on the stovetop. Turn frequently until skin is charred black. Transfer pepper to a plastic or paper bag, close the bag, and set aside for about 15 minutes. When the pepper is cool enough to handle, peel off the charred skin and discard the seeds, stem, and white membrane. Slice the pepper flesh into thin 1-inch-long strips and set them aside in the refrigerator. Carefully wash the spinach, discarding the stems. Dry the spinach leaves, tear them coarsely into bite-size pieces to measure 6 cups, and set aside in the refrigerator.

Heat a dry heavy-bottomed skillet over medium heat and toast the walnuts in it for about 5 minutes, shaking the pan frequently to toast evenly. When the walnuts are golden brown, place them in a small bowl and toss them with the lime juice while they are still warm. Sprinkle on the granulated garlic, chile powder, and ⅛ teaspoon of the salt and toss to distribute evenly. Set the walnuts aside.

Whisk together the orange juice, vinegar, olive oil, and the remaining ⅛ teaspoon salt. Toss together the spinach, onion, and orange juice mixture. Distribute evenly among 6 chilled serving plates. Distribute the red bell pepper strips among the plates, arranging them to one side of the greens. Sprinkle the salads with spiced nuts, then grind a little black pepper on each one, and distribute the cilantro evenly over the salads. Serve immediately.

━ ━━ ━ ━━ ━ ━━ ━ ━━ ━

Each serving provides:

94	Calories	7 g	Carbohydrate
4 g	Protein	203 mg	Sodium
7 g	Fat	0 mg	Cholesterol
3 g	Dietary Fiber		

Romaine and Radish Salad with Orange Anise Dressing

ALMOST INSTANT

This is a very refreshing salad, perfect with a meal such as Black Bean Enchiladas with Fresh Mint (page 194) or Corn and Cheese Tortilla Casserole with Grilled Tomato Sauce (page 200). You may use all romaine lettuce or a mix of fresh leafy greens.

Yield: 4 side-dish servings

Fresh-squeezed orange juice	2	**tablespoons**
Olive oil	1	**tablespoon**
Anise seeds	⅛	**teaspoon, crushed**
Ground cumin	⅛	**teaspoon**
Romaine lettuce leaves, torn	5	**cups**
Fresh red radishes	6	**large, thinly sliced**
Mild feta cheese, crumbled	1	**ounce (¼ cup)**

Whisk together the orange juice, olive oil, anise seeds, and cumin. Set aside at room temperature so the flavors can blend. Wash and dry the lettuce leaves and tear them into bite-size pieces to measure 6 cups. Place the lettuce in a large bowl along with the radishes and cheese. Toss to combine. Drizzle with the dressing, toss again, and serve.

━━━━━━━━━━━━━━━━

Each serving provides:

63	Calories	3 g	Carbohydrate
2 g	Protein	85 mg	Sodium
5 g	Fat	6 mg	Cholesterol
1 g	Dietary Fiber		

Soups and Stews

Hot and chunky stews, brimming with succulent ingredients, have been an important part of the cuisines of Meso-America since ancient times. Even today, many Mexican cooks wouldn't think of serving a meal without soup.

Soups and stews in Mexico can constitute the entire meal, with the addition of the ever-present hot tortillas and salsas. We have included many such hearty main-dish recipes in this chapter, along with lighter soups more suitable as first courses.

Whatever the weather, either north or south of the border, soups and stews are appetizing and nourishing. On the very hottest days, chilled or room temperature soups, such as Classic Gazpacho, make a refreshing repast. In the dead of winter, a substantial dish such as Green Pozole Stew warms, comforts, and satisfies.

This chapter presents meatless versions of some classic Mexican dishes plus a selection of our favorite new creations, designed to span the seasons.

Tips and Tools

- Good stock is the soul of good soups and stews. Making stock from scratch is a simple and satisfying experience, and homemade stock can be frozen for convenient future use. As an alternative, you may prepare stock from vegetable broth cubes. Individual recipes provide specific substitution instructions.
- When a recipe calls for puréeing a soup, be sure to do it in small batches to avoid splattering the hot liquid.
- The essential tools of soup-making are a large stockpot and a long-handled wooden spoon for stirring. You will need a ladle for serving, and pretty individual serving bowls. A tureen, though not essential, is the perfect serving vessel.

Green Pozole Stew

VEGAN

Pozole *is the Mexican term for cooked slaked corn kernels—what
we call hominy. Here is our vegetarian version of a classic Mexican
comfort food, made from convenient canned hominy. The flavors are
bold, the texture chunky and satisfying. Serve it with Mushroom and
Cheese Quesadillas (page 78) and a green salad for a wonderful lunch
or supper.*

Yield: 4 main-dish servings

Raw unsalted pumpkin seeds	½	**cup**
Fresh tomatillos	1	**pound (about 12 medium)**
Fresh serrano chiles	2	**medium**
Fresh sorrel leaves, chopped	½	**cup, firmly packed**
Mexican Vegetable Stock°	2½	**cups**
Garlic	1	**clove, chopped**
Canola oil	1	**tablespoon**
White hominy	1	**29-ounce can, drained (3 cups)**
Salt	¼	**teaspoon**

(continued)

°If you do not have Mexican Vegetable Stock on hand, make a batch according
to the directions on page 38, or dissolve 1 large low-sodium vegetable broth
cube in 2½ cups hot water.

Optional toppings
Minced white onion
Diced avocado tossed with lemon juice
Minced raw or pickled jalapeño chiles
Dried Mexican oregano
Diced fresh tomatoes
Minced fresh cilantro
Lime wedges for squeezing into the stew

Place the pumpkin seeds in a dry heavy-bottomed skillet over medium-high heat. Toast, shaking the pan occasionally, about 5 minutes. Seeds will brown and pop in the pan. Transfer to a plate or bowl to cool. When cool, grind the seeds with a mortar and pestle or in a food processor to a fine meal consistency. Set aside.

Meanwhile, remove and discard the husks of the tomatillos and wash them. Place the tomatillos in a saucepan, cover with water, and bring to a boil over high heat. Cover the pan, reduce the heat to medium, and cook 10 minutes. The tomatillos should be very soft. Drain them briefly and transfer them to a blender.

Remove and discard the stems of the chiles and scrape out the seeds for a milder dish. Add the chiles, sorrel, ½ cup of the stock, and the garlic to the blender and purée thoroughly.

Heat the oil in a heavy-bottomed, deep-walled pan over medium-high heat. Pour the tomatillo purée through a wire mesh strainer into the pan. Press with the back of a wooden spoon or rubber spatula to force the mixture through the mesh. Discard the tomatillo seeds that remain in the strainer. Cook the purée for 5 minutes, stirring frequently. Add the ground pumpkin seeds, reduce heat to low, and cook 10 minutes, occasionally stirring and scraping the bottom of the pan to prevent sticking.

Add the remaining 2 cups of stock, the hominy, and salt. Increase the heat to medium and cook 15 minutes, stirring occasionally. Meanwhile, prepare the toppings and place them in bowls to serve alongside the pozole. To serve, ladle hot soup into warmed bowls. Diners may add whatever combination of toppings they like.

Each serving provides:

290	Calories	36 g	Carbohydrate
11 g	Protein	807 mg	Sodium
13 g	Fat	0 mg	Cholesterol
3 g	Dietary Fiber		

Classic Gazpacho

VEGAN

Patsy Ford, a friend in Nevada City, first introduced this easy, but delicious recipe to us. Enjoy it for lunch or as a cool summer supper, with warmed corn tortillas or quesadillas.

Yield: 6 main-dish servings

Fresh tomatoes	2	**large (1 pound)**
Cucumber	1	**medium (½ pound)**
Red onion	1	**medium, minced**
Green bell pepper	1	**medium, minced**
Pimientos	1	**4-ounce jar, drained**
Tomato juice	1½	**cups**
Olive oil	2	**tablespoons**
Red wine vinegar	⅓	**cup**
Tabasco sauce	¼	**teaspoon**
Salt	½	**teaspoon**
Black pepper		**Several grinds**
Garlic	2	**cloves, minced**

Cut the tomatoes in half crosswise and squeeze gently over the sink to remove the juicy seed pockets. Cut out the stem ends, finely dice the tomatoes, and transfer them to a large bowl.

Peel the cucumber and cut it in half lengthwise. With a spoon, scrape out and discard the seeds. Finely dice the cucumber and add it to the tomatoes.

Add the red onion, bell pepper, and pimientos to the tomatoes and cucumbers. Place 1 cup of the tomato juice in a blender and spoon in a third of the tomato mixture. Purée until smooth then return to the bowl. Stir in the remaining ½ cup tomato juice and the oil, vinegar, Tabasco, salt, pepper, and garlic. Cover the bowl and chill for several hours before serving. Gazpacho will keep for a few days in the refrigerator.

Each serving provides:

85	Calories	10 g	Carbohydrate
2 g	Protein	408 mg	Sodium
5 g	Fat	0 mg	Cholesterol
2 g	Dietary Fiber		

Avocado Tomato Bisque

VEGAN

This velvety soup, which can be served either warm or chilled, is stunning. It makes an elegant first course when you are preparing a sit-down Mexican-inspired dinner party, or a satisfying summer lunch entrée, served with Mushroom and Cheese Quesadillas (page 78) and a leafy salad. It is most important to use perfectly ripe avocados for this dish.

Yield: 8 first-course servings

Fresh serrano chile	**1**	**medium**
Mexican Vegetable Stock*	**2½**	**cups**
Canned tomatoes, drained and chopped	**1**	**cup**
White onion	**½**	**medium, chopped**
Fresh epazote leaves, chopped	**¼**	**cup**
Ripe Haas avocados	**2**	**medium (1 pound)**
Fresh-squeezed lime juice	**2**	**tablespoons**
Salt	**½**	**teaspoon**
Pure chile powder	**½**	**teaspoon**
Fresh cilantro leaves, minced	**¼**	**cup**

*If you do not have Mexican Vegetable Stock on hand, make a batch according to the directions on page 38, or dissolve 1 large low-sodium vegetable broth cube in 2½ cups hot water.

Discard the stem of the chile and scrape out the seeds for a milder dish. Finely mince the chile. Combine the stock, tomatoes, onion, epazote, and chile in a medium saucepan. Bring to a strong simmer over high heat, then reduce heat to medium-low and simmer gently for 20 minutes. Transfer half of the mixture to a blender.

Cut open 1 of the avocados, and remove the pit (see page 6). Use a spoon to scrape the avocado out of the skin into the blender. Add 1 tablespoon of the lime juice and ¼ teaspoon of the salt and purée briefly, until smooth. Transfer the purée to a large bowl. Repeat the process with the remaining stock mixture, avocado, 1 tablespoon lime juice, and ¼ teaspoon salt, and add the purée to the bowl.

Transfer the soup to a tureen or to individual shallow serving bowls. Sprinkle the chile powder over the top and distribute the minced cilantro leaves among the bowls. Allow the soup to stand at room temperature until it cools to lukewarm. Alternatively, chill the soup for several hours, then remove it from the refrigerator and top it with the garnishes about 30 minutes before serving time.

Each serving provides:

85	Calories	7 g	Carbohydrate
2 g	Protein	207 mg	Sodium
7 g	Fat	0 mg	Cholesterol
1 g	Dietary Fiber		

Mushroom Purée with Cilantro and Ancho Chiles

This cream of mushroom soup delivers all the satisfaction of the classic version, though its base is vegetable stock rather than cream. Spiked with plenty of garlic, cilantro, and pungent ancho chiles, it is a delicious Mexican interpretation of a perennial favorite.

Yield: 6 first-course servings

Dried ancho chiles	2	**medium**
Russet potato	1	**medium (about ½ pound)**
Button mushrooms	¾	**pound**
Mexican Vegetable Stock*	3	**cups**
Half-and-half	½	**cup**
Dry sherry	¼	**cup**
Salt	½	**teaspoon**
Unsalted butter	1	**tablespoon**
White onion	1	**medium, finely chopped**
Fresh cilantro leaves, minced	1	**cup**
Garlic	4	**cloves, minced**
Ground cumin	1	**teaspoon**

Use your hands to tear the chiles into large pieces, discarding the seeds and stems. Place the chiles in a bowl and cover with 1 cup boiling water. Allow to soak about ½ hour. (Alternatively,

---

*If you do not have Mexican Vegetable Stock on hand, make a batch according to the directions on page 38, or dissolve 1 large low-sodium vegetable broth cube in 3 cups hot water.

you may soften the chiles by covering them with water and heating them in a microwave oven on the high setting for 1 to 3 minutes, depending on your particular oven.)

Meanwhile, peel and finely dice the potato. Brush or wipe the mushrooms clean and thinly slice them. Heat the stock to a boil over high heat in a large saucepan or stockpot. Add the reconstituted chiles along with their soaking liquid, the potato, and the mushrooms and return to a boil. Reduce the heat to medium and simmer about 15 minutes, until the potato is very tender.

Transfer half of the mixture to a blender and purée. Strain the purée back into the pan. Repeat this process with the remaining half. Add the half-and-half, sherry, and salt to the pan. Cook for 1 to 2 minutes over medium heat, but don't allow the soup to boil.

Meanwhile, melt the butter in a small skillet over medium-high heat. Add the onion and stir and sauté about 3 minutes, until it begins to soften. Add the cilantro, garlic, and cumin and sauté for 2 to 3 minutes longer.

Serve the soup very hot in shallow bowls, with a portion of the onion mixture mounded onto the center of each serving.

Each serving provides:

121	Calories	16 g	Carbohydrate
4 g	Protein	233 mg	Sodium
5 g	Fat	13 mg	Cholesterol
2 g	Dietary Fiber		

Tomato Soup with Fideos and Serrano Chiles

VEGAN

Yes, pasta is eaten in Mexico! Fideo, *or coiled vermicelli, is traditionally used in soup, but standard vermicelli may be substituted. The pasta is toasted in the oven before it is added, which gives the soup a distinctive flavor. This makes a fine, light main course, or you may serve it as a first course for 8 to 10 people.*

Yield: 6 main-dish servings

Dried fideos (coiled vermicelli)	7	**ounces**
Fresh tomatoes	2	**medium (about 1 pound)**
Yellow onion, diced	½	**cup**
Garlic	2	**cloves**
Mexican Vegetable Stock*	6	**cups**
Salt	¼	**teaspoon**
Fresh serrano chiles	2	**medium**

Preheat the oven to 400 degrees F. Break up the pasta slightly and place it on a large dry baking sheet. Toast it in the oven for 5 to 6 minutes, until lightly browned. Watch the time closely; if the pasta gets too dark, it will have a bitter flavor. Remove from the baking sheet and set aside.

Place the tomatoes, onion, and garlic in a food processor with ½ cup of water. Purée until smooth, then pour into a stockpot and heat to steaming over medium-high heat. Add the

---

*If you do not have Mexican Vegetable Stock on hand, make a batch according to the directions on page 38, or dissolve 2 large low-sodium vegetable broth cubes in 6 cups hot water.

toasted pasta and cook for about 3 minutes, stirring constantly, to slightly soften it. Add the stock and salt, increase the heat to high, and bring to a boil. Reduce the heat to medium, cover the pan, and continue to cook for 10 to 12 minutes, until the pasta is tender.

Meanwhile, remove and discard the stems of the chiles and scrape out the seeds for a milder dish. Finely mince the chiles. Spoon the soup into warmed shallow bowls and garnish with the chiles. Serve immediately.

Each serving provides:

154	Calories	31 g	Carbohydrate
6 g	Protein	151 mg	Sodium
1 g	Fat	0 mg	Cholesterol
2 g	Dietary Fiber		

Spinach and Corn Soup with Pastina and Smoked Cheese

This soup is simple and elegant—a lovely first course or luncheon entrée. Like a good French onion soup, it has a depth of flavor that is delectable. Use any tiny pasta shape—stars, alphabets, or circles. Any smoked cheese, such as cheddar, Swiss, or Edam, will work well in this soup.

Yield: 4 first-course servings

Fresh serrano chile	1	**medium**
Fresh spinach	¾	**pound (about 1 bunch)**
Unsalted butter	1	**tablespoon**
White onion	½	**medium, thinly sliced**
Mexican Vegetable Stock*	4	**cups**
Garlic	1	**clove, minced**
Pure chile powder	1	**teaspoon**
Salt	¼	**teaspoon**
Black pepper		**Several grinds**
Corn kernels, fresh or frozen**	1	**cup**
Dried pastina	½	**cup**
Smoked cheese	2	**ounces (½ cup)**
Dried Mexican oregano	1	**teaspoon**

*If you do not have Mexican Vegetable Stock on hand, make a batch according to the directions on page 38, or dissolve 1½ large low-sodium vegetable broth cubes in 4 cups hot water.

**If you are using fresh corn, you will need about 2 medium ears to yield 1 cup kernels.

Remove and discard the stem of the chile and scrape out the seeds for a milder dish. Finely mince the chile and set aside.

Carefully wash the spinach leaves, discarding the stems. Finely chop the spinach leaves and set them aside. Melt the butter in a large saucepan or stockpot over medium heat. Sauté the onion with the chile until the onion is just beginning to brown, about 5 minutes. Add the stock, garlic, chile powder, salt, and pepper and bring to a simmer over medium-high heat. Add the corn and pastina, reduce the heat to medium, and simmer for 10 minutes, stirring frequently to prevent the pastina from sticking to the bottom of the pan. Add the spinach and gently stir it into the soup until wilted and well incorporated.

Place a portion of the cheese in each of 4 warmed shallow bowls. Ladle the hot soup over the cheese, and crumble ¼ teaspoon of dried oregano over each serving. Serve immediately.

Each serving provides:

222	Calories	29 g	Carbohydrate
9 g	Protein	468 mg	Sodium
9 g	Fat	23 mg	Cholesterol
4 g	Dietary Fiber		

Cream Soup with Tequila-Sautéed Peppers and Fresh Tomato

Simple yet satisfying, this soup will become a family favorite. Corn-bread with Whole Kernels (page 98) makes a terrific accompaniment. The poblanos add more flavor than heat, while the tomato lends fresh flavor and bright color. Panela cheese is available in some Mexican markets, but Jack cheese is a fine substitute.

Yield: 6 main-dish servings

Fresh poblano chiles	2	**large (½ pound)**
Green bell pepper	1	**large (½ pound)**
Unsalted butter	2	**tablespoons**
Yellow onion, diced	½	**cup**
Gold tequila	¼	**cup**
Mexican Vegetable Stock*	4	**cups**
Unbleached flour	3	**tablespoons**
Lowfat milk	4	**cups**
Salt	¼	**teaspoon**
Part-skim panela cheese, shredded	4	**ounces (1 cup)**
Fresh tomato	1	**large, chopped**

Remove and discard the stem, seeds, and membranes of the chile and bell pepper and finely dice them. Melt the butter in a heavy-bottomed skillet over medium heat. Add the chile, bell

*If you do not have Mexican Vegetable Stock on hand, make a batch according to the directions on page 38, or dissolve 1½ large low-sodium vegetable broth cubes in 4 cups hot water.

pepper, and onion; sauté for 3 minutes, then stir in the tequila. Continue to sauté for about 8 minutes, until the vegetables are fork-tender.

Meanwhile, place all but ½ cup of the stock in a large stockpot over medium-high heat. Put the reserved ½ cup of the stock in a jar that has a tight-fitting lid; add the flour and shake to dissolve. Whisk the flour mixture into the stock and bring to a boil. Cook for 4 to 5 minutes, then add the milk and heat to a simmer, stirring frequently. Add the sautéed vegetables and salt and continue to cook until heated through, but not boiling.

Place equal portions of cheese and tomato in the bottom of each of 6 warmed soup bowls. Ladle soup into bowls and serve immediately.

Each serving provides:

236	Calories	21 g	Carbohydrate
12 g	Protein	332 mg	Sodium
12 g	Fat	33 mg	Cholesterol
2 g	Dietary Fiber		

Corn Chowder with Ancho Chiles, Okra, and Cream

Here is a marvelously rich-tasting soup, satisfying as a main course for lunch. A good cornbread and a tart salad would fill out the meal nicely. Make this during the late summer months, when corn and okra are at their peak and are least expensive.

Yield: 6 main-dish servings

Dried ancho chiles	2	**medium**
Canned pear tomatoes, drained	1	**cup**
White onion, diced	½	**cup**
Mexican Vegetable Stock**	2¾	**cups**
Unsalted butter	1	**tablespoon**
Fresh okra	½	**pound**
Corn kernels, fresh or frozen*	3	**cups**
Dried Mexican oregano	2	**teaspoons**
Salt	½	**teaspoon**
Fresh cilantro leaves, finely minced	2	**tablespoons**
Heavy cream	2	**tablespoons**

*If you're using fresh corn, you will need about 6 medium ears to yield 3 cups of kernels.

**If you do not have Mexican Vegetable Stock on hand, make a batch according to the directions on page 38, or dissolve 1 large low-sodium vegetable broth cube in 2¾ cups of hot water.

Use your hands to tear the chiles into large pieces, discarding the seeds and stems. Place the chiles in a bowl and cover with 2 cups boiling water. Allow to soak about ½ hour. (Alternatively, you may soften the chiles by covering with water and heating them in a microwave oven on the high setting for 1 to 3 minutes, depending on your particular oven.)

Meanwhile, place the tomatoes in a blender and purée them. When the chiles are softened, drain and add to the blender, along with the onion and 1 cup of the stock. Purée until smooth and homogenous, about 1 minute. Set aside.

Melt the butter over medium heat in a heavy-bottomed, high-walled pan. Before the butter starts to brown, add the tomato mixture and cook 5 minutes, stirring frequently. The sauce will sizzle as it cooks and reduce just a bit. Rinse and dry the okra pods, discard the stems, and cut crosswise into ¼-inch slices.

Meanwhile, place 2 cups of the corn and ¾ cup of the stock in a blender. Blend for 1 to 2 minutes, until smoothly puréed. Add the corn purée to the reduced tomato sauce, along with the remaining 2 cups stock, 1 cup whole corn kernels, the okra, oregano, and salt. Bring to a simmer over medium-high heat, then reduce heat to medium-low and simmer 10 to 15 minutes, stirring frequently, until the corn and okra are tender but not mushy. Stir in the cilantro and cream and serve immediately.

Each serving provides:

175	Calories	32 g	Carbohydrate
6 g	Protein	290 mg	Sodium
5 g	Fat	13 mg	Cholesterol
5 g	Dietary Fiber		

Rice and Garbanzo Soup with Chipotle Chiles, Avocado, and Tomato

ALMOST INSTANT, VEGAN

The chipotles called for in this recipe are sold in cans labeled chile chipotle en salsa de adobo. They have a moderate heat and a smoky flavor that is incomparable. Remove the seeds when you mince the chiles, if you prefer a milder dish.

Yield: 4 main-dish servings

Olive oil	1	**tablespoon**
Garlic	2	**cloves, minced**
Yellow onion, diced	½	**cup**
Carrot, diced	¾	**cup**
Mexican Vegetable Stock*	6	**cups**
Uncooked long-grain white rice	½	**cup**
Chipotle chiles en adobo, minced	2	**teaspoons**
Dried Mexican oregano	1	**teaspoon**
Salt	¼	**teaspoon**
Cooked garbanzo beans**	1	**cup, drained**
Fresh-squeezed lime juice	2	**tablespoons**
Ripe Haas avocado	1	**medium (about ½ pound)**
Fresh tomato	1	**large, chopped**

*If you do not have Mexican Vegetable Stock on hand, make a batch according to the directions on page 38, or dissolve 2 large low-sodium vegetable broth cubes in 6 cups hot water.

**Cook dried beans according to the instructions on page 31, or purchase canned beans that do not contain additives.

Heat the oil over medium heat in a stockpot and add the garlic, onion, and carrot. Sauté for 2 to 3 minutes, then add the stock, rice, chile, oregano, and salt. Increase the heat to high and bring the stock to a boil, then reduce to low and cook about 15 to 20 minutes, stirring occasionally, until the rice is tender. Add the garbanzo beans and continue to cook for 5 minutes to heat them through. Stir in the lime juice and remove the pan from the heat.

Cut open the avocado and remove the pit (see page 6). Peel and dice the avocado. Evenly distribute the avocado and tomato in the bottom of 4 warmed soup bowls and ladle the soup over them. Serve immediately.

Each serving provides:

380	Calories	61 g	Carbohydrate
9 g	Protein	236 mg	Sodium
12 g	Fat	0 mg	Cholesterol
4 g	Dietary Fiber		

Split Pea Soup with Yam and Mexican Seasonings

VEGAN

This nourishing soup makes a marvelous winter meal. The sweetness of the yam and the bright flavor of lime juice give it a delicate quality not usually associated with split pea soup. Small dollops of Mexican Crema (page 33) and Guacamole (page 88) set off the soup nicely, but it's quite delicious without them.

Yield: 4 main-course servings

Olive oil	1	**tablespoon**
White onion	1	**medium, diced**
Dried rosemary	1	**teaspoon, crushed**
Dried thyme	¼	**teaspoon, crushed**
Pure chile powder	2	**tablespoons**
Mexican Vegetable Stock°	7½	**cups**
Dried green split peas	1	**cup**
Salt	½	**teaspoon**
Red-skinned yam	¾	**pound (about 1 large)**
Garlic	4	**cloves, minced**
Fresh cilantro leaves, minced	⅓	**cup**
Fresh-squeezed lime juice	2	**tablespoons**

°If you do not have Mexican Vegetable Stock on hand, make a batch according to the directions on page 38, or dissolve 2 large low-sodium vegetable broth cubes in 7½ cups hot water.

Heat the oil in a stockpot over medium heat and add the onion, rosemary, and thyme. Sauté, stirring almost constantly, for 3 minutes, then add the chile powder. Stir and cook for another minute to toast the chile powder a bit, then add the stock, split peas, and salt. Bring to a simmer over high heat, then reduce the heat to medium and simmer 15 minutes.

Meanwhile, peel the yam and chop it into ¼-inch dice. After the soup has simmered 15 minutes, add the yam along with the garlic. Bring back to a simmer, and cook, stirring frequently, 15 to 20 minutes, until the split peas and sweet potato are tender. Stir in the cilantro and lime juice and serve very hot, topped with dollops of guacamole and crema, if desired.

Each serving provides:

348	Calories	63 g	Carbohydrate
15 g	Protein	421 mg	Sodium
5 g	Fat	0 mg	Cholesterol
7 g	Dietary Fiber		

Black Bean Soup with Epazote and Lime

VEGAN

This black bean soup gains its unique flavor from epazote, the pungent herb dear to the hearts of many Mexican cooks. Epazote lends a mysterious depth of flavor that is quite delicious.

Yield: 4 main-dish servings

Dried black beans	1	cup
Mexican Vegetable Stock*	8	cups
Red bell pepper	1	medium
Canola oil	2	tablespoons
Yellow onion	1	medium, diced
Celery	2	ribs, chopped
Garlic	3	cloves, minced
Cumin seeds	1	teaspoon
Coriander seeds	1	teaspoon
Dried Mexican oregano	1	teaspoon
Pure chile powder	1	teaspoon
Bay leaves	2	medium
Black pepper	¼	teaspoon
Fresh epazote leaves, minced	2	tablespoons
Fresh-squeezed lime juice	2	tablespoons
Salt	½	teaspoon

Rinse and sort the beans, put them in a large stockpot, and cover with boiling water. Cover the pot and allow the beans to soak for about 1 hour. Drain into a colander. Return the beans to the

*If you do not have Mexican Vegetable Stock on hand, make a batch according to the directions on page 38, or dissolve 2 large low-sodium vegetable broth cubes in 8 cups hot water.

stockpot and add the vegetable stock. Bring them to a boil over high heat, reduce the heat to medium-low, and simmer, uncovered, 30 minutes.

Meanwhile, remove the seeds, stem, and white membranes from the bell pepper and finely dice the flesh. Heat the oil in a large heavy-bottomed skillet over medium heat and sauté the bell pepper, onion, celery, garlic, cumin, coriander, oregano, chile powder, and bay leaves for 10 minutes. Add the sautéed vegetables to the beans and continue to cook for 30 minutes. Add the black pepper, epazote, lime juice, and salt and continue to cook for about 15 minutes, until the beans are tender. Serve immediately.

— ▬ ▬ ▬ ▬ ▬ ▬ ▬ —

Each serving provides:

283	Calories	42 g	Carbohydrate
13 g	Protein	399 mg	Sodium
8 g	Fat	0 mg	Cholesterol
8 g	Dietary Fiber		

Vegetable Soup with Fried Tortilla Strips and Avocado Salsa

VEGAN

A study in textures and temperatures, this soup is pretty and interesting enough to serve as the first course at an elegant dinner party. It has three components, two of which can be done hours in advance.

Yield: 6 first-course servings

Ripe Haas avocado	1	medium (about ½ pound)
Salsa Cruda (page 54)	1	cup
Fresh-squeezed lime juice	2	teaspoons
Canola or safflower oil for frying tortilla strips *		
Corn tortillas, fresh or slightly stale	4	standard-size
Zucchini	1	medium (about ⅓ pound)
Canola oil	1	tablespoon
White onion	½	large, diced
Yellow or red bell pepper	½	medium, minced
Pure chile powder	1	teaspoon
Fresh cilantro leaves, minced	¼	cup
Garlic	1	clove, minced
Button mushrooms	¼	pound, sliced

*Amount of oil needed varies, depending on the size of the pan used. Nutritional data includes 1 tablespoon of oil, which is the amount absorbed by the tortillas during frying.

Mexican Vegetable Stock*	4	cups
Salt	¼	teaspoon
Cooked black beans**	2	cups, drained
Shelled peas, fresh or frozen	⅓	cup

Cut open the avocado and remove the pit (see page 6). Peel and dice the avocado. Combine the avocado in a bowl with the salsa and lime juice and set aside.

Pour canola oil into a high-walled, heavy-bottomed pan to a depth of about 3 inches and heat over medium heat. Cut the tortillas in half and cut each half into ¼-inch wide strips. After the oil has been heating for 2 minutes or so, drop a tortilla strip into the oil. If it begins to sizzle furiously, the oil is hot enough. If it doesn't, keep heating the oil, testing every minute or so, until the right sizzling temperature is achieved. (If the oil is not hot enough, the tortilla strips will absorb a great deal of oil and will not become crisp.)

If you are using a small pan, cook the tortilla strips in small amounts. Fry the strips in the hot oil for 2 to 3 minutes, until they are lightly browned and quite crisp. It is fine if they curl up. Place the fried tortilla strips on layers of paper towels for a few minutes to drain off excess oil, then remove them from the towels and set aside on a plate. This much can be done well ahead of time. Hold the fried tortilla strips at room temperature.

(continued)

*If you do not have Mexican Vegetable Stock on hand, make a batch according to the directions on page 38, or dissolve 1½ large low-sodium vegetable broth cubes in 4 cups hot water.

**Cook dried beans according to the instructions on page 31, or purchase canned beans that do not contain additives.

About 30 minutes before serving time, discard the ends of the zucchini and slice it crosswise as thinly as you can to create delicate rounds. Heat 1 tablespoon of canola oil in a heavy-bottomed sauté pan or small stockpot. Add the onion, bell pepper, and chile powder and stir and sauté until the onion is transparent and limp, about 4 minutes. Stir in the cilantro and garlic, then the mushrooms and zucchini. Stir until everything is well distributed, then add the stock and salt. Bring to a simmer over high heat, then reduce the heat to medium and simmer 10 minutes. Stir in the beans and peas and cook for about 2 minutes, until just heated through.

Place a portion of the tortilla strips in the bottom of each of 6 shallow warmed soup bowls. Ladle a portion of the hot soup over the tortilla strips, and top each serving with a portion of the avocado mixture. Serve immediately, before the tortilla strips become soggy.

Each serving provides:

255	Calories	34 g	Carbohydrate
9 g	Protein	198 mg	Sodium
11 g	Fat	0 mg	Cholesterol
6 g	Dietary Fiber		

Potato, Zucchini, and Olive Stew with Garlic, Jalapeños, and Tomatoes

VEGAN

This rich and delicious Mexican flavor combination develops through long, slow cooking. The technique, however, is quite simple. The recipe calls for fresh tomatoes. If they are not in season, you may substitute one 28-ounce can of whole tomatoes, drained, and omit the roasting step. Select the smallest potatoes you can find—any variety, or a combination of varieties, will work. For a hearty meal, serve the stew with plain or Mexican-flavored rice, Cornbread with Whole Kernels (page 98), and a tart green salad.

Yield: 6 main-dish servings

Fresh tomatoes	4	**pounds (about 8 medium)**
Olive oil	3	**tablespoons**
Garlic	10	**cloves**
White onion	½	**medium**
Mexican Vegetable Stock*	1½	**cups**
Fresh parsley leaves, chopped	1	**cup**
Salt	⅛	**teaspoon**
Whole baby potatoes	1¼	**pounds**
Zucchini	3	**medium (1 pound)**
Whole pimiento-stuffed olives	1	**cup, drained**
Pickled jalapeño chiles, minced	2	**teaspoons**

*If you do not have Mexican Vegetable Stock on hand, make a batch according to the directions on page 38, or dissolve ½ of a large low-sodium vegetable broth cube in 1½ cups hot water.

Roast the tomatoes on a hot grill or under a preheated broiler, turning frequently, until their skins are well charred, about 20 minutes. Remove from the heat and set aside to cool for a few minutes. When the tomatoes are cool enough to handle, cut out the stem ends, peel away and discard most of the blackened skin, and place the tomatoes in a blender.

Meanwhile, heat the oil over medium heat in a heavy-bottomed stockpot or deep Dutch oven. Add the whole garlic cloves and cook, stirring constantly, until they begin to turn golden brown. This will take only 1 to 2 minutes. Watch carefully—if the garlic gets too dark, it will taste bitter. Turn off the heat. Remove the garlic cloves from the oil with a slotted spoon and add them to the tomatoes in the blender, along with the onion, stock, parsley, and salt. Purée until smooth.

Strain the purée through a fine mesh strainer into the pan in which the garlic was cooked. Press with the back of a wooden spoon or rubber spatula to remove as much liquid as possible. Discard the seeds that remain in the strainer. Bring the tomato purée to a simmer over medium-high heat, reduce the heat to very low, and simmer, stirring frequently, 20 minutes. The sauce will reduce considerably.

Meanwhile, cook the whole potatoes in plenty of rapidly boiling water until they are barely fork-tender, 10 to 15 minutes, depending on their size. Drain and set aside. Discard the stems and root ends of the zucchini and slice them crosswise into rounds ½ inch thick.

After the sauce has simmered 20 minutes, cut the potatoes in half and stir them into the sauce, along with the zucchini, olives, and chiles. Simmer over low heat, stirring frequently, 20 minutes. Serve very hot.

Each serving provides:

243	Calories	36 g	Carbohydrate
6 g	Protein	655 mg	Sodium
10 g	Fat	0 mg	Cholesterol
9 g	Dietary Fiber		

Lentil Stew with Pineapple and Banana

VEGAN

In the Oaxaca region of Mexico, tropical fruits are plentiful and often show up in interesting combinations. Here the earthy flavor of the lentils are complemented by the sweetness of the pineapple and banana. When buying fresh pineapple, pick one with a strong, sweet fragrance. It can be held at room temperature, unpeeled and uncut, for a few days before using.

Yield: 6 main-dish servings

Dried brown lentils	2	**cups**
Mexican Vegetable Stock*	8	**cups**
Fresh pineapple, chopped	1	**cup**
Canola oil	2	**tablespoons**
White onion	1	**medium, diced**
Garlic	2	**cloves**
Banana	1	**large, sliced**
Ground coriander	½	**teaspoon**
Ground cumin	½	**teaspoon**
Salt	¼	**teaspoon**
Black pepper		**Several grinds**
Green onions	3,	**minced**

*If you do not have Mexican Vegetable Stock on hand, make a batch according to the directions on page 38, or dissolve 2 large low-sodium vegetable broth cubes in 8 cups hot water.

Rinse and sort the lentils, then place them in a stockpot with the stock. Bring to a boil over high heat, then lower to medium, cover, and simmer for 20 to 25 minutes, until the lentils are tender but not mushy. Drain the lentils, reserving the cooking liquid.

Cut the pineapple in half crosswise and slice off the leafy top. Use a sharp knife to peel the pineapple and remove and discard the tough core portion. Dice some of the pineapple to measure 1 cup and reserve the rest for another use.

Heat the oil in the stockpot over medium heat and add the white onion and garlic. Sauté for 2 to 3 minutes, then stir in the cooked lentils, pineapple, banana, coriander, cumin, salt, and pepper. Add 2 cups of the reserved bean cooking liquid, increase the heat to high, and bring the stew to a boil. Cover, reduce the heat to medium-low, and simmer about 30 minutes, stirring occasionally. Stir the green onions into the soup and continue to cook for about 5 minutes, to just soften the onions. Serve immediately.

━ ━━ ━ ━━ ━ ━━ ━ ━━ ━ ━

Each serving provides:

318	Calories	51 g	Carbohydrate
19 g	Protein	167 mg	Sodium
6 g	Fat	0 mg	Cholesterol
9 g	Dietary Fiber		

Tortilla Dishes

Tortillas are the humble and wholesome heart of Mexican cuisine, present at every meal and used in a variety of ways. Plain or buttered fresh tortillas are enjoyed much as bread is in other countries, used to push food onto the fork and to sop up savory juices from the plate before it is eaten, down to the last crumb.

Other times, tortillas are incorporated into the dish, as in enchiladas and tacos. In traditional Mexican kitchens, nothing is wasted—slightly stale tortillas are fried to become *tostaditas*, what we know as tortilla chips, or are cooked into casseroles or soups, where they add texture as well as flavor.

You may opt to make fresh corn tortillas from masa harina (see page 42) or from fresh masa. They have a delicious flavor and texture that the packaged varieties can't duplicate, though the latter may certainly be used with good results in our recipes that call for corn tortillas.

Flour tortillas, which are favored in this book for use in quesadillas, burritos, and fajitas, are a traditional staple of northern Mexico. Our recipes call for packaged fresh flour tortillas in one of the three sizes commonly available at supermarkets.

Tips and Tools

- For best results with tortilla dishes, use the freshest tortillas you can find, or make your own (see page 42). Tortillas that are stale, dry, or brittle are not well-suited to the recipes in this chapter—use them for chips or in casseroles.

- To soften tortillas without resorting to oil-frying, heat them briefly using one of the methods described on page 30 before using them in recipes.

- Many Mexican cookbooks suggest serving enchiladas immediately after rolling them, topped with hot sauce. However, we prefer to heat the finished enchiladas briefly in the oven so they can be served piping hot.

- When making enchiladas, it is wise to have extra tortillas on hand in case of breakage.

- For optimal flavor and authenticity, we fry fresh corn tortillas for crisp tacos and tostadas. People who are accustomed to using a commercial brand of crisp taco or tostada shells may substitute them, if they wish.

- An inexpensive tortilla press will form balls of masa into the appropriate pancake-like shape with very little time or effort. A good press may be made of either wood or metal, but it must be heavy and sturdy; such a tortilla press will last a lifetime. Look for one at kitchen supply stores or Mexican specialty markets.

- Standard glass baking dishes are recommended for cooking enchiladas and other baked tortilla dishes.
- Special pans are available for cooking fajitas, but we find we can achieve excellent results using a well-seasoned cast-iron skillet.
- Whole wheat flour tortillas are often available at natural food stores and at some supermarkets. They may be used in any of our recipes that call for flour tortillas.

Spinach and Crema Enchiladas with Ancho Chile Mole

The ancho chile is a dried poblano that has a smoky, spicy sweetness. These enchiladas are light and flavorful, and the sauce is utterly delicious.

Yield: 8 enchiladas

Garlic	1	**large bulb**
Dried ancho chiles	3	**medium**
Fresh tomato	1	**large (about ½ pound)**
White onion	1	**small, diced**
Dried Mexican oregano	1	**teaspoon**
Ground cinnamon	⅛	**teaspoon**
Ground cloves		**A pinch**
Salt	¼	**teaspoon**
Mexican Vegetable Stock*	1	**cup**
Corn tortillas	8	**standard-size**
Fresh spinach	1½	**pounds (about 2 bunches)**
Raw unsalted pumpkin seeds	¼	**cup, finely chopped**
Mexican Crema (page 33)	½	**cup**

(continued)

---

*If you do not have Mexican Vegetable Stock on hand, make a batch according to the directions on page 38, or dissolve ½ of a large low-sodium vegetable broth cube in 1 cup of hot water.

Preheat the oven to 375 degrees F. Cut ¼-inch off the top of the garlic bulb to barely expose the tops of the cloves. Do not peel. Use a clay garlic baker or wrap in foil and bake for 30 to 45 minutes, until the garlic bulb is very soft. Remove from the oven and set aside to cool, reducing the oven temperature to 350 degrees F. When cool enough to handle, remove the garlic from the skin by squeezing the cloves from the bottom. The garlic will slide out the cut end as a soft paste.

Meanwhile, use your hands to tear open the ancho chiles, discarding the seeds and stems. Place the chiles in a bowl and cover with 2 cups of boiling water. Allow them to soak for about 30 minutes. (Alternatively, you may soften the chiles by covering them with water and heating them in a microwave oven for 1 to 3 minutes, depending on your particular oven.) Drain well.

Meanwhile, core the tomato and quarter it. Place it in a food processor along with the baked garlic, reconstituted chiles, onion, oregano, cinnamon, cloves, and salt. Purée until smooth. Transfer to a saucepan and stir in the stock. Cook over medium heat, stirring frequently, for about 10 minutes, until slightly reduced.

Warm the tortillas (see page 30) and wrap in a clean towel to keep warm. While the sauce is cooking, make the filling. Carefully wash the spinach and discard the stems. Coarsely chop the leaves and place them in a large pan, without drying them. Cover and steam over medium heat until the spinach wilts, about 5 minutes. Drain into a colander, pressing the spinach with the back of a wooden spoon to remove as much water as possible. Transfer to a bowl and stir in the pumpkin seeds and crema.

Spread a third of the sauce on the bottom of a 7½ × 12-inch glass or ceramic baking dish and set it on your work surface, along with a clean dinner plate. Set the spinach filling nearby. If necessary, reheat the remaining sauce over medium-low heat until it is steaming hot but not simmering, and place it near your work surface.

Working with 1 tortilla at a time, briefly immerse it in the sauce to coat it lightly. Place the tortilla on the plate and put about an eighth of the spinach filling in a narrow, even heap across the tortilla, slightly off-center. Loosely roll up and place seam side down in the baking dish.

When the remaining tortillas are filled, rolled, and placed snugly in the baking dish, pour all of the remaining sauce over them, including any sauce that has collected on the plate. Cover the dish and bake for 15 to 20 minutes to heat through, then allow to stand 5 minutes before serving.

Each enchilada provides:

216	Calories	30 g	Carbohydrate
8 g	Protein	219 mg	Sodium
9 g	Fat	21 mg	Cholesterol
6 g	Dietary Fiber		

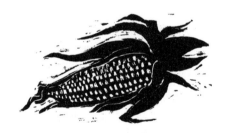

Chayote and Red Potato Fajitas

ALMOST INSTANT, VEGAN

Fajitas are a fun food to serve and eat—it's a real hands-on experience. These are particularly good served with Smooth Tomatillo Salsa (page 60) and Lowfat Crema (page 34).

Yield: 4 main-dish servings

Fresh serrano chiles	2	medium
Red potatoes	1	pound
Chayotes	2	medium (1 pound)
Flour tortillas*	8	fajita-size
Olive oil	2	tablespoons
Fresh-squeezed lime juice	¼	cup
Honey	1	tablespoon
Garlic	2	cloves, minced
Ground cumin	¼	teaspoon
Ground coriander	¼	teaspoon
Pure chile powder	¼	teaspoon

Remove and discard the stems of the chiles and scrape out the seeds for a milder dish. Finely mince the chiles and set aside.

Scrub the potatoes and cut them into bite-size cubes. Place in a saucepan and cover with water. Bring to a boil over high heat and cook until just fork-tender, but not falling apart, about 8 minutes. Drain well. Meanwhile, cut the chayotes into matchsticks, discarding the seeds. Set aside.

Warm the tortillas (see page 30). In a small bowl, whisk together the olive oil, lime juice, honey, chiles, garlic, cumin, cori-

---

*Some brands of flour tortillas are made with lard. Read the labels and select a lard-free variety.

ander, and chile powder. Pour into a fajita pan or cast-iron skillet and heat over medium-high heat until barely simmering. Add the potatoes and chayotes and toss them as they cook 7 to 10 minutes. The liquid will cook away and the vegetables will char just slightly. Transfer to the table in the pan, steaming hot. Pass the tortillas and allow each diner to fill them with vegetables. Serve with your favorite condiments or those mentioned in the recipe introduction.

Each serving provides:

426	Calories	70 g	Carbohydrate
10 g	Protein	77 mg	Sodium
12 g	Fat	0 mg	Cholesterol
6 g	Dietary Fiber		

Tostadas with Roasted Nopalitos

Prickly pear cactus paddles are a common vegetable in Mexico, where they are called nopales or nopalitos. In this dish, roasting the nopales lends a delicious, smoky flavor, which is nicely complemented by the fresh papaya.

Yield: 12 tostadas

Fresh serrano chile	1	**medium**
Fresh pear tomatoes	1	**pound**
Fresh papaya	1	**pound (about 1 large)**
Green onions	3	**minced**
Fresh cilantro leaves, minced	¼	**cup**
Fresh-squeezed lime juice	¼	**cup**
Salt	½	**teaspoon**
Fresh nopales	1	**pound**
Canola oil for frying*		
Corn tortillas	12	**standard-size**
Fresh red radishes	4	**medium**
Refried Black Beans (page 290)	2	**cups (1 recipe)**
Part-skim queso fresco, crumbled	2	**ounces (½ cup)**

Remove and discard the stem of the chile and scrape out the seeds for a milder dish. Finely mince the chile and set aside.

Remove and discard the stem ends of the tomatoes. Cut the tomatoes in half crosswise and gently squeeze them over the sink to remove the juicy seed pockets. Chop the tomatoes and

---

*Amount of oil needed varies, depending on the size of the pan used. Nutritional data includes 2 tablespoons of oil, which is the amount absorbed by the tortillas during frying.

place them in a bowl. Remove and discard the skin and seeds from the papaya. Chop the papaya and place it in the bowl with the tomatoes and green onions. Add the cilantro and chile and toss to combine. In a small bowl, whisk together the lime juice and salt. Pour over the tomato mixture and set aside.

Use the back side of a knife to scrape any thorns off the nopales, taking care not to stick yourself. Do not remove the peel, however. Lay the nopales flat on your work surface, and cut off and discard ¼-inch of the outer rim and the base end. Heat a cast-iron skillet over high heat and add the nopales. Cook, turning occasionally, for about 8 to 10 minutes, until they are slightly charred. Remove them from the skillet and allow to cool slightly. Cut lengthwise into thin strips, then into about 1-inch pieces. Place in a bowl and set aside.

Pour canola oil into a small heavy-bottomed skillet to a depth of about ¼ inch. When the oil is hot enough to sizzle a drop of water, add the tortillas, 1 at a time, and fry them until crisp, about 2 minutes per side. Transfer to layers of paper towels to drain off excess oil, then stack the crisp tortillas on a plate or in a basket. You may add more oil, if necessary, but be sure to heat it sufficiently before frying the next tortilla.

Thinly slice the radishes and place in a small bowl. Reheat the refried beans, if necessary, and put them in a serving bowl. Place the cheese in a serving bowl. Place the tomato mixture, nopalitos, radishes, and cheese on the table. Pass the crisp corn tortillas, allowing each diner to top theirs first with beans, then the tomato mixture, some nopalitos, radish slices, and finally a bit of cheese.

Each tostada provides:

188	Calories	29 g	Carbohydrate
7 g	Protein	183 mg	Sodium
6 g	Fat	3 mg	Cholesterol
4 g	Dietary Fiber		

Refried Beans and Chorizo Tostadas

Tostadas are a great idea for a casual dinner party or for snacks when friends have gathered for an afternoon. The chorizo takes some advance planning, but the rest can come together quickly if you use canned vegetarian refried beans and commercial salsa fresca. Diners spread beans and chorizo on the crisp tortillas, then help themselves to the fixings.

Yield: 12 tostadas

Ripe Haas avocados	2	**medium (1 pound)**
Fresh-squeezed lime juice	2	**tablespoons**
Green cabbage, finely shredded	2	**cups**
Muenster cheese, shredded	4	**ounces (1 cup)**
Mild feta cheese, crumbled	4	**ounces (1 cup)**
Salsa Cruda (page 54)	1½	**cups**
Canola oil for frying		
Corn tortillas	12	**standard-size**
Simple Refritos with Onion and Oregano (page 286)	3	**cups**
Tofu Chorizo Sausage (page 40)	3	**cups**

Cut open the avocados and remove the pits (see page 6). Peel and dice the avocados, then toss them with the lime juice in a

---

*The amount of oil needed varies, depending on the size of the pan used. Nutritional data includes 2 tablespoons, which is the amount absorbed by the oil during frying.

bowl. Set out on the table. Also set out the cabbage, cheeses, and salsa in separate serving bowls.

Pour canola oil into a small heavy-bottomed skillet to a depth of about ¼ inch. When the oil is hot enough to sizzle a drop of water, add the tortillas, 1 at a time, and fry them until crisp, about 2 minutes per side. Transfer to layers of paper towels to drain off excess oil, then stack the crisp tortillas on a plate or in a basket. You may add more oil, if necessary, but be sure to heat it sufficiently before frying the next tortilla.

Reheat the beans and chorizo, if necessary. Place the tortillas, beans, and chorizo on the table and instruct diners to create their own tostadas, starting with a layer of beans, then the chorizo, then the toppings of their choice.

▬ ▬ ▬ ▬ ▬ ▬ ▬ ▬

Each tostada provides:

466	Calories	54 g	Carbohydrate
19 g	Protein	529 mg	Sodium
21 g	Fat	17 mg	Cholesterol
9 g	Dietary Fiber		

Soft Tacos with Tofu and Pickled Jalapeños

ALMOST INSTANT, VEGAN

Serve these deliciously spicy soft tacos with a commercially prepared salsa, or our Salsa Fresca (page 56) or Salsa Cruda (page 54). Lowfat Crema (page 34) also makes a tasty accompaniment.

Yield: 10 tacos

Extra-firm tofu	1	**pound**
Canola oil	2	**tablespoons**
Yellow onion	1	**medium, diced**
Garlic	2	**cloves, minced**
Cumin seeds	2	**teaspoons**
Pure chile powder	1	**teaspoon**
Dried Mexican oregano	1	**teaspoon**
Dried thyme	½	**teaspoon**
Black pepper	⅛	**teaspoon**
Canned tomato sauce	½	**cup**
Pickled jalapeño chiles, minced	2	**teaspoons**
Corn tortillas	10	**standard-size**
Fresh tomatoes, diced	2	**medium (about 1 pound)**
Green leaf lettuce, finely shredded	2	**cups**

Drain the tofu and cut into ½-inch slices. Blot dry on a tea towel, then crumble into a bowl and mash. Heat the oil over medium-high heat in a large heavy-bottomed skillet and add the onion, garlic, cumin, chile powder, oregano, thyme, and black pepper. Sauté for about 2 minutes then add the tomato sauce and chiles. Add the tofu and continue to cook for 3 to 5 minutes, stirring frequently, until heated through.

Meanwhile, warm the tortillas (see page 30) and wrap them in a clean tea towel to keep them warm. Arrange the tomatoes and lettuce on a serving platter. Mound the tofu mixture in a warm bowl. Transfer all the ingredients to the table and serve at once, allowing diners to fill their own tacos.

Each taco provides:

178	Calories	20 g	Carbohydrate
9 g	Protein	141 mg	Sodium
7 g	Fat	0 mg	Cholesterol
3 g	Dietary Fiber		

Soft Tacos with Cumin-Braised Acorn Squash

Cumin and winter squash make an unusual and delicious taco filling when combined with the heat of the chiles and the pungency of the cilantro.

Yield: 12 tacos

Uncooked long-grain white rice	½	**cup**
Fresh serrano chiles	2	**medium**
Acorn squash	1	**medium (about 1½ pounds)**
Cumin seeds	1	**tablespoon**
Mexican Vegetable Stock*	1	**cup**
Corn tortillas	12	**standard-size**
Fresh cilantro leaves, minced	½	**cup**
Part-skim queso fresco, crumbled	4	**ounces (1 cup)**

Bring 1 cup of water to a boil in a small saucepan. Add the rice and return to a boil. Reduce the heat to low, cover the pan, and cook 20 minutes. Remove from the heat and set aside with the lid in place.

Remove and discard the stems of the chiles and scrape out the seeds for a milder dish. Finely mince the chiles and set aside. Cut the squash in half lengthwise and scoop out the seeds.

*If you do not have Mexican Vegetable Stock on hand, make a batch according to the directions on page 38, or dissolve ½ of a large low-sodium vegetable broth cube in 1 cup of hot water.

Peel each half, then cut into 1-inch cubes. Coarsely crush the cumin seeds with a mortar and pestle.

Place the stock in a skillet and heat over medium-high heat. Stir in the cumin and chiles. Add the squash, cover the pan, and cook for 12 to 15 minutes, until the squash is fork-tender. Stir occasionally during the cooking time.

Meanwhile, warm the tortillas (see page 30) and wrap them in a clean tea towel to keep them warm. When the squash is tender and the liquid has been absorbed, stir in the rice and cilantro. Transfer to a warm serving dish. Serve the filling with warm tortillas and the cheese, allowing diners to create their own tacos.

Each taco provides:

141	Calories	24 g	Carbohydrate
5 g	Protein	121 mg	Sodium
3 g	Fat	5 mg	Cholesterol
3 g	Dietary Fiber		

Roasted Pepper, Black Bean, and Avocado Tacos with Bleu Cheese

The bleu cheese is a decidedly unconventional touch in these delicious summer tacos. If you have cooked beans on hand—either thawed from an earlier frozen batch or canned—all the cooking that is required is briefly toasting the spices, heating the tortillas, and roasting the bell pepper. And the pepper-roasting step can be eliminated by using the roasted red bell peppers that are sold in jars at every supermarket. You will need 1 cup of thin, short pepper strips.

Yield: 8 tacos

Red bell pepper	1	medium
Ripe Haas avocado	1	medium (about ½ pound)
Fresh-squeezed lime juice	2	tablespoons
Cooked black beans*	1	cup, drained
White onion, diced	½	cup
Coriander seeds	1	teaspoon
Dried Mexican oregano	2	teaspoons
Pure chile powder	1	teaspoon
Salt	⅛	teaspoon
Bleu cheese, crumbled	1	ounce (¼ cup)
Corn tortillas	8	standard-size
Green leaf lettuce, finely shredded	1½	cups

*Cook dried beans according to the instructions on page 31, or purchase canned beans that do not contain additives.

Wash and dry the bell pepper. Place the whole pepper on a hot grill, under a preheated broiler, or directly onto a gas burner on the stovetop. Turn the pepper every few minutes until the skin is charred almost uniformly black. Transfer the pepper to a plastic or paper bag and fold the bag closed. Set aside at room temperature. The steam in the bag will finish cooking the pepper. When the pepper is cool enough to handle, peel off the charred skin, discard the seeds, stem, and white membranes, and cut the flesh into narrow, short strips. Place the pepper strips in a bowl.

Cut open the avocado and remove the pit (see page 6). Peel and dice the avocado. Add the avocado to the pepper strips in the bowl, along with the lime juice. Toss gently to combine. Add the beans and onion and toss again.

Thoroughly crush the coriander seeds with a mortar and pestle. Place the coriander, oregano, and chile powder in a small dry skillet over medium heat and toast, stirring constantly, for 1 to 2 minutes. Add the toasted spices to the avocado mixture, along with the salt and bleu cheese. Toss gently to combine and set aside at room temperature.

Warm the tortillas (see page 30) and wrap them in a clean tea towel to keep them warm. Transfer the avocado mixture, shredded lettuce, and tortillas to the table and allow diners to fill their own tacos.

Each taco provides:

153	Calories	23 g	Carbohydrate
5 g	Protein	181 mg	Sodium
5 g	Fat	3 mg	Cholesterol
3 g	Dietary Fiber		

Tortilla Dishes

Mushroom and Corn Tacos with Serrano Chiles and Epazote

ALMOST INSTANT, VEGAN

This is a delightful combination of traditional flavors. Except for the epazote, it is made from easy-to-find ingredients that are available year-round. If fresh epazote is impossible to find, you may substitute fresh cilantro, or simply omit the herb altogether. These delicious tacos come together very quickly—you'll want to make them often.

Yield: 8 tacos

Button mushrooms	³⁄₄	**pound**
Fresh serrano chiles	2	**medium**
Canola oil	1	**tablespoon**
White onion, minced	¹⁄₃	**cup**
Garlic	2	**cloves, minced**
Corn kernels, fresh or frozen*	1	**cup**
Salt	¹⁄₄	**teaspoon**
Fresh epazote leaves, minced	2	**tablespoons**
Corn tortillas	8	**standard-size**
Green cabbage, finely shredded	1¹⁄₂	**cups**

Wipe or brush the mushrooms clean and quarter them, stems and all. Set aside. Remove the stems from the chiles, along with the seeds for a milder dish. Finely mince the chiles and set aside.

Heat the oil over medium heat in a heavy-bottomed skillet that has a tight-fitting lid. Sauté the chiles, onion, and garlic, stirring frequently, until the onion begins to go limp, about 3 min-

*If you are using fresh corn, you will need about 2 medium ears to yield 1 cup kernels.

utes. Add the quartered mushrooms and sauté an additional minute, stirring frequently, to brown them a bit. Stir in the corn, salt, and epazote. Holding the lid of the skillet in one hand, pour 2 tablespoons of water into the pan and immediately put the lid in place. Reduce the heat to low and cook 10 minutes. Remove the lid and continue to cook 1 to 2 minutes, if necessary, until there is no more than a tablespoon of liquid remaining in the pan.

Meanwhile, heat the tortillas (see page 30) and wrap them in a clean tea towel to keep them warm. Transfer the mushroom mixture to a serving bowl and put it on the table, along with the cabbage and tortillas. Serve immediately, inviting diners to make their own tacos. Your favorite salsas may be offered as optional toppings, if you wish.

Each taco provides:

126	Calories	23 g	Carbohydrate
4 g	Protein	133 mg	Sodium
3 g	Fat	0 mg	Cholesterol
3 g	Dietary Fiber		

Potato and Chorizo Tacos

VEGAN

Here is a vegetarian version of a traditional combination—potatoes and spicy sausage. Our chorizo sausage is made from tofu, and even die-hard sausage fans agree that it's a delicious facsimile. Make a batch of the chorizo up to a day or two ahead of time and these tacos can come together almost instantly.

Yield: 12 tacos

Red or white potatoes	¾	**pound**
Canola oil	1	**tablespoon**
White onion	1	**medium, diced**
Pure chile powder	2	**teaspoons**
Salt	¼	**teaspoon**
Tofu Chorizo Sausage (page 40)	1½	**cups**
Corn tortillas	12	**standard-size**
Green leaf lettuce, finely shredded	2	**cups**
Salsa Cruda (page 54)	2	**cups**

Without peeling them, finely dice the potatoes. Heat the oil over medium heat in a heavy-bottomed skillet that has a tight-fitting lid. Sauté the onions and chile powder for about 3 minutes, then add the potatoes and salt and sauté them, stirring frequently, 5 minutes. Holding the lid of the skillet in one hand, pour ½ cup of water into the pan and immediately put the lid in place. Reduce the heat to low and cook 10 minutes.

Remove the lid, stir in the chorizo, and continue to cook a minute or two, until the potatoes are tender and there is no more than a tablespoon of liquid remaining in the pan. If the liquid has evaporated and the potatoes are not yet tender, add another 1 to 2 tablespoons of water and continue to cook, covered, about 5 minutes, or until the potatoes are tender.

Meanwhile, warm the tortillas according to the instructions on page 30. Wrap them in a clean tea towel to keep them warm. Transfer the potato and chorizo filling to a serving bowl. Place the filling, tortillas, lettuce, and salsa on the table and serve immediately, allowing diners to create their own tacos.

Each taco provides:

149	Calories	25 g	Carbohydrate
5 g	Protein	227 mg	Sodium
4 g	Fat	0 mg	Cholesterol
3 g	Dietary Fiber		

Burritos with Spinach, Artichokes, Roasted Peppers, and Feta Cheese

These burritos are a family favorite, flavorful enough to please the adult palate, but mild enough to be enjoyed by children. Serve with Salsa Fresca (page 56) and Guacamole (page 88), if you wish. Because it uses such a small quantity of roasted red bell pepper, this recipe calls for the commercially prepared variety. You may, of course, roast a fresh pepper instead.

Yield: 8 burritos

Uncooked long-grain white rice	½	cup
Fresh parsley leaves, minced	¼	cup
Olive oil	1	tablespoon
Artichoke hearts, water packed	1	6-ounce jar
Fresh spinach	1½	pounds (about 2 bunches)
Roasted red bell pepper, chopped	½	cup
Fresh marjoram leaves, minced	2	tablespoons
Flour tortillas*	8	burrito-size
Mild feta cheese, crumbled	4	ounces (1 cup)

*Some brands of flour tortillas are made with lard. Read the labels and select a lard-free variety.

Bring 1 cup of water to a boil in a medium saucepan. Stir in the rice, parsley, and olive oil. Cover, reduce heat to very low, and cook 20 minutes. Remove saucepan from the heat and set aside, leaving the lid in place.

Drain the artichoke hearts and cut them into bite-size pieces. Carefully wash the spinach, discarding the stems. Pile the wet leaves into a saucepan, cover and cook over medium heat until the spinach wilts, about 5 minutes. Drain in a colander, pressing with a wooden spoon to remove as much water as possible. Transfer the spinach to a cutting board and coarsely chop it. Return it to the warm pan, along with the artichoke hearts, red bell pepper, marjoram, and cooked rice. Stir to combine.

Meanwhile, warm the tortillas (see page 30) and wrap them in a clean tea towel to keep them warm.

Just before serving, lay the tortillas flat on individual serving plates. Evenly divide the spinach mixture between the tortillas and top with equal amounts of the cheese. Fold the ends of each tortilla over the filling and roll closed. Serve immediately.

Each burrito provides:

311	Calories	43 g	Carbohydrate
11 g	Protein	351 mg	Sodium
10 g	Fat	13 mg	Cholesterol
5 g	Dietary Fiber		

Burritos with Potatoes, Pinto Beans, and Guacamole

VEGAN

For a wonderful brunch, we like to accompany these burritos with a garnish of fresh melon slices and a side of salsa. Serve with fresh citrus juice, beer, or margaritas.

Yield: 4 burritos

Russet potatoes	1½	**pounds (3 medium)**
Canola oil	1	**tablespoon**
Dried thyme	1	**teaspoon**
Dried marjoram	1	**teaspoon**
Green onions, minced	3	**medium**
Cooked pinto beans*	1	**cup, drained**
Ripe Haas avocados	2	**medium (1 pound)**
Garlic	1	**clove, minced**
Fresh-squeezed lemon juice	2	**tablespoons**
Salt	¼	**teaspoon**
Cayenne		**A pinch**
Red onion, finely minced	1	**tablespoon**
Fresh pear tomato	1	**medium, finely chopped**
Fresh cilantro leaves, minced	1	**tablespoon**
Flour tortillas**	4	**burrito-size**

*Cook dried beans according to the instructions on page 31, or purchase canned beans that do not contain additives.

**Some brands of flour tortillas are made with lard. Read the labels and select a lard-free variety.

Scrub the potatoes and peel and finely chop them. Put them in a saucepan and cover with cold water. Bring to a boil over high heat, reduce the heat to medium-high, and simmer 5 minutes, until the potatoes are barely fork-tender, but not falling apart. Drain into a colander.

Put the oil in a large skillet and heat over medium heat. Add the thyme, marjoram, and green onions. Cook for about 2 minutes to soften the onion, then add the potatoes. Sauté for 15 minutes, tossing occasionally, until they are lightly browned. Add the pinto beans and heat through for about 5 minutes.

Cut the avocado open and remove the pit (see page 6). With a spoon, scrape the avocado out of the skin into a bowl. Add the garlic, lemon juice, salt, and cayenne and mash together with a fork to create a fairly smooth texture. Add the red onion, tomato, and cilantro and stir well. Let the flavors blend at room temperature while you finish the burritos.

Warm the tortillas (see page 30) and wrap them in a clean tea towel to keep them warm. Just before serving, lay the tortillas flat on individual warmed serving plates. Evenly divide the potato mixture among the tortillas. Fold the ends of each tortilla over the filling and roll closed. Top each with a portion of the guacamole and serve immediately, with salsa on the side, if desired.

Each burrito provides:

618	Calories	89 g	Carbohydrate
18 g	Protein	218 mg	Sodium
22 g	Fat	0 mg	Cholesterol
11 g	Dietary Fiber		

Grilled Vegetable and Rice Burritos

VEGAN

Everyone loves to wrap their hands around a big burrito, and this one is sure to be a crowd-pleaser. The grilled vegetables and the chipotle chile lend a delicate smoky flavor to this dish. If you like, double the amount of chipotle chile for a more spicy filling.

Yield: 6 burritos

Uncooked long-grain brown rice	½	**cup**
Yellow onions	2	**medium**
Olive oil	2	**tablespoons**
Zucchini	3	**medium (1 pound)**
Red bell pepper	2	**large (1 pound)**
Flour tortillas*	6	**burrito-size**
Fresh-squeezed lime juice	2	**tablespoons**
Chipotle chiles en adobo, minced	1	**teaspoon**
Red cabbage, shredded	1½	**cups**

Bring 1 cup of water to a boil in a small saucepan. Add the rice and return to a boil. Reduce the heat to very low, cover the pan, and cook 45 minutes. Remove the pan from the heat and set aside, leaving the lid in place.

Meanwhile, preheat a coal or gas grill to high, 400 to 450 degrees F. Trim off the ends of the onions and peel them.

---

*Some brands of flour tortillas are made with lard. Read the labels and select a lard-free variety.

Cut them in half crosswise and lightly brush the cut sides with some of the olive oil. Place the onions on the grill cut ends down. Cover the grill and cook for about 35 minutes, turning every 8 to 10 minutes to cook them evenly. The onions are done when they are soft and slightly charred.

Meanwhile, remove the ends from the zucchini and cut them lengthwise into 3 strips. Lightly brush with a bit of the olive oil. Cut the bell peppers in half, discard the stems, seeds, and white membranes, then slice each half into thirds lengthwise. Brush with some of the olive oil. Place the zucchini and peppers on the grill and cook 15 to 20 minutes, turning several times while cooking. They will char slightly and become limp. Warm the tortillas (page 30) and wrap them in a clean tea towel to keep them warm.

Remove all of the vegetables from the grill and allow them to cool slightly, then coarsely chop them. Place them in a medium bowl and add the rice. Toss to combine. Add the lime juice and chile to any remaining olive oil and whisk together. Drizzle over the grilled vegetable mixture and toss to combine.

Just before serving, lay the tortillas flat on individual warmed serving plates. Evenly divide the grilled vegetable mixture and cabbage among the tortillas. Fold the ends of each tortilla over the filling and roll closed. Serve immediately.

Each burrito provides:

336	Calories	52 g	Carbohydrate
9 g	Protein	71 mg	Sodium
10 g	Fat	0 mg	Cholesterol
6 g	Dietary Fiber		

Cheese Enchiladas with Green Chile Mole

These simple and elegant enchiladas are a wonderful, creamy treat. Serve them with Lowfat Crema (page 34) and Smooth Ancho Chile Salsa (page 64), or your favorite condiments.

Yield: 12 enchiladas

Coriander seeds	2	teaspoons
Canned whole mild green chiles	2	4-ounce cans, drained
Fresh cilantro leaves, chopped	1⅓	cups
Mexican Vegetable Stock*	2	cups
Raw unsalted pumpkin seeds	½	cup
White onion, diced	1½	cups
Garlic	3	cloves, minced
Granulated sugar	1	teaspoon
Salt	¼	teaspoon
Black pepper		Several grinds
Canola oil	1	tablespoon
Corn tortillas	12	standard-size
Muenster cheese, shredded	8	ounces (2 cups)
Mild feta cheese, crumbled	4	ounces (1 cup)

*If you do not have Mexican Vegetable Stock on hand, make a batch according to the directions on page 38, or dissolve ½ large low-sodium vegetable broth cube in 2 cups of hot water.

Preheat the oven to 350 degrees F. Crush the coriander seeds thoroughly in a mortar and pestle. In a blender, combine the green chiles, 1 cup of the cilantro, the stock, pumpkin seeds, ½ cup of the onion, the garlic, coriander, sugar, salt, and pepper. Purée thoroughly. Heat the oil in a heavy-bottomed skillet and add the purée. Bring to a simmer over medium-high heat, then reduce the heat to medium-low and simmer gently, stirring frequently, 15 minutes.

Meanwhile, warm the tortillas (see page 30) and wrap them in a clean tea towel to keep them warm. In a bowl, toss together the cheeses, the remaining 1 cup onion, and the remaining ⅓ cup cilantro. Spread ½ cup of the sauce over the bottom of a 9 × 13-inch glass or ceramic baking dish and place it on your work surface, along with a clean dinner plate. Set the cheese filling nearby. If necessary, briefly heat up the remaining sauce over medium-low heat until it is steaming hot but not simmering, and place near your work surface.

Working with 1 tortilla at a time, briefly immerse it in the sauce to coat it lightly. Place the tortilla flat on the plate and, with your hands, place about ¼ cup of the cheese filling in a narrow, even heap across the tortilla, slightly off-center. Loosely roll up the tortilla and place it seam side down in the dish.

When all of the tortillas have been filled, rolled, and placed snugly in the baking dish, pour all of the remaining sauce over them, including any that has collected on the plate. Cover the dish and bake for 15 to 20 minutes to heat through, then allow to stand at room temperature 5 minutes before serving.

Each enchilada provides:

222	Calories	19 g	Carbohydrate
10 g	Protein	468 mg	Sodium
12 g	Fat	26 mg	Cholesterol
2 g	Dietary Fiber		

Potato and Zucchini Enchiladas with Red Chile Sauce

Since both sauce and filling can be made ahead of time, enchiladas are a great dinner party main course. Get the enchiladas assembled and into the oven, then quickly prepare a simple Mexican rice and a salad dressing, to be added to mixed greens just before serving. Set out spiced pumpkin seeds and a bowl of olives as appetizers. You might even have a few minutes to relax before your guests arrive. This hearty dish, with its classic ranchero-type sauce, has won rave reviews at every recipe testing.

Yield: 12 enchiladas

Russet potatoes	1	pound (about 2 medium)
Fresh jalapeño chile	1	small
Garlic	5	cloves
Zucchini	2	medium (¾ pound)
Canola oil	3	tablespoons
White onion	½	medium, diced
Cumin seeds	1	teaspoon
Romano cheese, finely grated	⅓	cup
Mild feta cheese, crumbled	2½	ounces (⅔ cup)
Dried New Mexico chiles	10	medium
Mexican Vegetable Stock*	2½	cups

*If you do not have Mexican Vegetable Stock on hand, make a batch according to the directions on page 38, or dissolve 1 large low-sodium vegetable broth cube in 2½ cups of hot water.

Salt	1/2	teaspoon
Corn tortillas	12	standard-size
Unbleached flour	3	tablespoons
Apple cider vinegar	2	teaspoons
Dried Mexican oregano	2	teaspoons
Bay leaf	1	large

Peel and dice the potatoes and steam for 10 to 15 minutes, until barely fork-tender. Meanwhile, remove and discard the stem of the jalapeño and scrape out the seeds for a milder dish. Finely mince the chile and set it aside in a small dish.

Mince 2 of the garlic cloves and set aside. Trim off the ends of the zucchini and dice them. Heat 1 tablespoon of the oil over medium heat in a heavy-bottomed skillet that has a tight-fitting lid. Sauté the zucchini and onion 10 minutes, stirring frequently. Add the minced garlic, the cumin, jalapeño, potatoes, and 1/4 cup of water. Cover and cook 5 minutes longer. Set aside. Combine the cheeses in a bowl and set aside.

Use your hands to tear the New Mexico chiles open, discarding the seeds and the stems. Place the chiles in a bowl and cover with 8 cups of boiling water. Allow to soak about 30 minutes. (Alternatively, you may soften the chiles by covering them with water and heating them in a microwave oven 1 to 3 minutes, depending on your particular oven.) Drain the chiles and place them in a blender with the stock, the remaining 3 whole cloves of garlic, and salt. Purée thoroughly.

Preheat the oven to 350 degrees F. Warm the tortillas (see page 30) and wrap them in a clean tea towel to keep them warm.

(continued)

Heat the remaining 2 tablespoons oil over medium heat in a heavy-bottomed skillet. Add the flour and stir constantly until lightly browned, about 2 minutes. Strain the chile purée into the pan and add the vinegar, oregano, and bay leaf. Cook, stirring frequently, about 10 minutes over medium heat, until somewhat thickened. Remove the bay leaf and discard.

Spread ½ cup of the sauce over the bottom of a 9 × 13-inch glass or ceramic baking dish and place the dish on your work surface, along with a clean dinner plate. Place the filling nearby. If necessary, reheat the remaining sauce over medium-low heat until it is steaming hot but not simmering, and place it near your work surface.

Working with 1 tortilla at a time, briefly immerse it in the sauce to coat it lightly. Place the tortilla on the plate and, with your hands, place a portion of the filling in a narrow, even heap across the tortilla, slightly off-center. Add 1 tablespoon of the cheese mixture and roll the tortilla up loosely around the filling. Place seam side down in the baking dish.

When all the tortillas have been filled, rolled, and placed snugly in the dish, pour all of the remaining sauce over them, including any sauce that has collected on the plate. Distribute the remaining cheese mixture over the top, cover, and bake 15 to 20 minutes to heat through. Allow to stand 5 minutes before serving.

Each enchilada provides:

203	Calories	32 g	Carbohydrate
6 g	Protein	255 mg	Sodium
6 g	Fat	7 mg	Cholesterol
4 g	Dietary Fiber		

Eggplant Enchiladas with Almond Mole

VEGAN

Though mole *translates loosely to "sauce" or "mixture," most of us think immediately of the traditional mole poblano, a dark and rich sauce made with sweet as well as savory spices, nuts, and cocoa. For the purposes of this book, we use* mole *to mean any sauce that is richer and more complex than an ordinary gravy or salsa. This mole is based on almonds seasoned with anise and allspice—an utterly delicious combination with the eggplant and raisin filling. This special dish is fit for company.*

Yield: 12 enchiladas

Whole blanched almonds	1¼	**cups**
Green bell pepper	1	**medium**
Eggplants	2	**pounds (about 2 small)**
Canola oil	1½	**tablespoons**
White onions	1½	**medium, diced**
Carrot	1	**medium, diced**
Garlic	6	**cloves, minced**
Salt	½	**teaspoon**
Cumin seeds	1	**teaspoon**
Golden raisins	¼	**cup, chopped**
Corn tortillas	12	**standard-size**
Dried ancho chiles	2	**medium**
Mexican Vegetable Stock*	2½	**cups**
Canned whole pear tomatoes	4	

*If you do not have Mexican Vegetable Stock on hand, make a batch according to the directions on page 38, or dissolve 1 large low-sodium vegetable broth cube in 2½ cups of hot water.

Allspice berries	**4**	
Anise seeds	½	teaspoon
Coriander seeds	½	teaspoon

Preheat the oven to 350 degrees F. Spread the almonds out on a dry baking sheet. Bake for 15 to 20 minutes, stirring once or twice during this time, until the almonds are light tan in color. Remove almonds from the baking sheet and set aside at room temperature. Leave the oven on.

Dice the bell pepper, discarding the stem, seeds, and white membranes. Set aside. Slice off and discard the stem ends of the eggplants and, without peeling them, cut the eggplant into ½-inch cubes. Heat 1 tablespoon of the oil over medium heat in a large heavy-bottomed skillet. Sauté 1 onion, along with the bell pepper and carrot for 3 minutes, then add the eggplant, 4 cloves of the minced garlic, and ¼ teaspoon of the salt. Crush the cumin seeds thoroughly with a mortar and pestle and stir them into the eggplant. Sauté, stirring frequently, 10 to 15 minutes, until the eggplant and carrot are tender. Meanwhile, finely chop ¼ cup of the toasted almonds. Stir the raisins and chopped almonds into the eggplant mixture and set aside.

Warm the tortillas (see page 30) and wrap them in a clean tea towel to keep them warm. Heat a dry heavy-bottomed skillet or cast-iron griddle over medium-high heat. Use your hands to tear the chiles into large pieces, discarding the seeds and stems. Place the chile pieces on the hot griddle and toast for 1 to 2 minutes, occasionally pressing down on them with a spatula. They should blister a bit and begin to lighten in color. Turn them over and toast the other side briefly.

When the chiles are lightly toasted, place them in a blender. Add the remaining 1 cup toasted almonds, along with the stock, tomatoes, and the remaining ½ onion, 2 cloves minced garlic, and ¼ teaspoon salt. Coarsely crush the allspice berries and anise seeds with a mortar and pestle and add them to the blender. Purée the mixture thoroughly. Heat the remaining ½ tablespoon oil in a heavy-bottomed skillet and add the purée. Cook over medium heat, stirring frequently, for 5 minutes. Set aside near your work surface.

Spread ½ cup of the sauce evenly over the bottom of a 9 × 13-inch glass or ceramic baking dish and place it on your work surface, along with a clean dinner plate. Set the eggplant filling nearby. If necessary, reheat the remaining sauce until it is steaming hot but not simmering, and place it near your work surface.

Working with 1 tortilla at a time, briefly immerse it in the sauce to coat it lightly. Place it on the plate and, with your hands, place a portion of the filling in a narrow, even heap across the tortilla, slightly off center. Loosely roll the tortilla up around the filling and place the enchilada seam side down in the baking dish.

When all of the tortillas have been filled, rolled, and placed snugly in the baking dish, pour all of the remaining sauce over them, including any sauce that has collected on the plate. Cover and bake 15 to 20 minutes to heat through. Allow to stand 5 minutes before serving.

Each enchilada provides:

278	Calories	31 g	Carbohydrate
8 g	Protein	179 mg	Sodium
15 g	Fat	0 mg	Cholesterol
6 g	Dietary Fiber		

Black Bean Enchiladas with Fresh Mint

The mint adds a fresh, light note to these hearty enchiladas, which are simple to prepare and utterly delicious!

Yield: 8 enchiladas

Canola oil	2	**tablespoons**
Yellow onion	1½	**medium, chopped**
Celery	1	**stalk, chopped**
Garlic	4	**cloves, minced**
Chipotle chiles en adobo, minced	1	**tablespoon**
Dried Mexican oregano	1	**teaspoon**
Ground cinnamon	¼	**teaspoon**
Ground cloves		**A pinch**
Salt	¼	**teaspoon**
Black pepper		**Several grinds**
Mexican Vegetable Stock＊	2	**cups**
Tomato paste	1	**cup**
Corn tortillas	8	**standard-size**
Dark rum	4	**tablespoons**
Ground cumin	½	**teaspoon**
Pure chile powder	1	**teaspoon**
Cooked black beans＊＊	2	**cups, drained**

＊If you do not have Mexican Vegetable Stock on hand, make a batch according to the directions on page 38, or dissolve ½ of a large low-sodium vegetable broth cubes in 2 cups of hot water.

＊＊Cook dried beans according to the instructions on page 31, or purchase canned beans that do not contain additives.

Bean cooking or canning		
liquid	2	tablespoons
Fresh mint leaves, minced	¼	cup
Part-skim queso fresco,		
crumbled	6	ounces
		(1½ cups)

Heat 1 tablespoon of the oil in a large heavy-bottomed skillet over medium heat and add ½ of a diced onion, the celery, and 2 cloves of the garlic. Sauté for 5 minutes, then stir in the chile, oregano, cinnamon, cloves, salt, and pepper. Whisk in the stock and tomato paste, increase the heat to medium-high, and cook 5 minutes, whisking frequently. Transfer to a blender and purée until smooth. Return to the skillet and set aside.

Preheat the oven to 350 degrees F. Warm the tortillas (see page 30) and wrap them in a clean tea towel to keep them warm. Heat the remaining 1 tablespoon oil over medium heat in another large skillet and add the remaining chopped onion and the remaining 2 cloves garlic. Stir in 2 tablespoons of the rum, the cumin, and chile powder. Sauté for 3 to 4 minutes, until the onions are tender.

Meanwhile, place the beans in a medium bowl and add the cooking liquid, and mash the black beans slightly. Add the mashed beans, the mint, and the remaining 2 tablespoons rum to the onion mixture in the skillet. Stir and heat through for about 1 minute.

Spread ½ cup of the sauce over the bottom of a 7½ × 12-inch baking dish and place the dish on your work surface, along with a clean dinner plate. Place the filling nearby. Briefly heat up the remaining sauce, if necessary, until steaming hot but not simmering, and place it near your work surface.

(continued)

Working with 1 tortilla at a time, briefly immerse it in the sauce to coat it lightly. Place the tortilla on the plate and place an eighth of the bean mixture in a narrow, even heap across the tortilla, slightly off-center. Top with about 3 tablespoons of the cheese. Loosely roll up the tortilla and place it seam side down in the baking dish. Proceed until you have filled all the tortillas in this manner.

When all of the tortillas are filled, rolled, and placed snugly in the baking dish, spoon the remaining sauce over the top, including any sauce that has collected on the plate. Cover the dish and bake for 15 to 20 minutes to heat through. Allow to stand for 5 minutes before serving.

Each enchilada provides:

271	Calories	34 g	Carbohydrate
12 g	Protein	545 mg	Sodium
9 g	Fat	11 mg	Cholesterol
6 g	Dietary Fiber		

Chard and Poblano Chile Enchiladas with Tomatillo Sauce

The tomatillo sauce is the perfect complement to the chard and poblano chiles, creating an enchilada that is elegant enough to serve at a gourmet dinner. Try them accompanied by the Tortilla Chip Salad with Lime Shallot Dressing (page 116).

Yield: 8 enchiladas

Fresh tomatillos	¾	pound (9 medium)
Serrano chiles	2	medium
Cumin seeds	1	teaspoon
Canola oil	3	tablespoons
Yellow onion, chopped	¾	cup
Garlic	4	cloves, minced
Ground cinnamon	¼	teaspoon
Mexican Vegetable Stock*	1	cup
Fresh cilantro leaves, minced	¼	cup
Fresh poblano chiles	2	medium (½ pound)
Swiss chard	1	pound
Corn tortillas	8	standard-size
Salt	¼	teaspoon
Mild feta cheese, crumbled	6	ounces (1½ cups)

*If you do not have Mexican Vegetable Stock on hand, make a batch according to the directions on page 38, or dissolve ½ of a large low-sodium vegetable broth cube in 1 cup of hot water.

Remove and discard the husks of the tomatillos, rinse them, and place in a saucepan. Cover with water and bring to a boil over high heat. Reduce the heat to medium, cover the pan, and simmer about 10 minutes, until the tomatillos are very tender. Drain and place them in a food processor. Pulse to chop them and leave in the food processor and set aside.

Remove and discard the stems of the serrano chiles and scrape out the seeds for a milder dish. Finely mince the chiles. Crush the cumin seeds thoroughly with a mortar and pestle. Place 2 tablespoons of the oil in a small skillet and heat over medium-high heat. Add ½ cup of the onion, 2 cloves of the garlic, the serrano chiles, cinnamon, and half of the crushed cumin seeds. Sauté for several minutes, until the onion is tender. Add to the tomatillos in the food processor and pulse to combine. Place the mixture back into the skillet over medium-high heat and whisk in the stock. Cook about 5 minutes, until slightly thickened, then add the cilantro. Remove from the heat and set aside.

Meanwhile roast the poblano chiles on a hot grill or under the broiler for about 5 minutes, until the skin is charred. Turn and blacken the other side. Put them in a paper or plastic bag. Close the bag and set aside at room temperature; the steam inside the bag will finish cooking the peppers. When they are cool enough to handle, remove and discard the skin, stem, and seeds. Chop the chiles and set aside.

Preheat the oven to 350 degrees F. Wash the chard leaves well, but do not dry them. Thinly slice the stems and coarsely chop the leaves; set the stems and leaves aside separately. Warm the tortillas (see page 30) and wrap them in a clean tea towel to keep them warm. Heat the remaining 1 tablespoon oil in a heavy-bottomed stockpot over medium heat. Add the remaining ¼ cup onion, 2 cloves garlic, and the remaining crushed cumin seeds and sauté for a moment, then stir in the chard stems and salt. Sauté for 5 minutes, then mound the wet greens on top, cover tightly, and cook an additional 5 minutes. Remove the lid, and stir the wilted greens to combine with the other ingredients in the stockpot. Add the chopped poblano chiles and continue to cook for about 5 minutes, stirring occasionally, until all the liquid has evaporated. Remove from the heat.

Spread about a third of the tomatillo sauce evenly over the bottom of a 7½ × 12-inch glass baking dish and place it on your work surface, along with a clean dinner plate. Reheat the remaining sauce over medium-low until hot but not simmering, and place it near your work surface.

Working with 1 tortilla at a time, gently slide it into the sauce to coat it lightly. Place on a plate and put about an eighth of the chard mixture in a narrow, even heap across the center of the tortilla, slightly off-center. Top this with about an eighth of the cheese. Loosely roll up each enchilada and place it seam side down in the dish. When all of the tortillas are filled, rolled, and placed snugly in the baking dish, pour all the remaining sauce over the top, including any sauce that has collected on the plate. Cover and bake for 15 to 20 minutes to heat through. Allow to stand 5 minutes before serving.

━━━━━━━━━━━━━━━━━━━━

Each enchilada provides:

217	Calories	24 g	Carbohydrate
7 g	Protein	438 mg	Sodium
11 g	Fat	19 mg	Cholesterol
4 g	Dietary Fiber		

Corn and Cheese Tortilla Casserole with Grilled Tomato Sauce

The grilled tomatoes contribute a rich smoky flavor to this simple sauce. Serve the casserole with Spicy Green Rice (page 260) and cold beer.

Yield: 6 main-dish servings

Fresh pear tomatoes	2½	**pounds**
Fresh poblano chiles	6	**large (1½ pounds)**
Fresh or slightly stale corn tortillas	8	**standard-size**
Canola oil	⅛	**teaspoon**
Corn kernels, fresh or frozen*	2	**cups**
Part-skim queso fresco, crumbled	4	**ounces (1 cup)**

Preheat a coal or gas grill to medium-high. Slice off the stem ends from the tomatoes, but leave them whole. Place the tomatoes on the grill and cook for about 30 minutes, turning several times to just char the skin evenly. At the same time, place the chiles on the grill and cook them 5 minutes, until their skins blacken. Turn and char the other side. Place the chiles in a paper or plastic bag, fold the bag closed, and set aside at room temperature. When cool enough to handle, remove and discard the skin, stem, and seeds. Cut the chiles into long, thin strips and set aside. Put the grilled tomatoes in a food processor and purée.

*If you are using fresh corn, you will need about 4 medium ears to yield 2 cups of kernels.

Preheat the oven to 350 degrees F. Cut the tortillas all the way across into 1-inch strips. Rub a 2 quart casserole dish with the oil and spread a third of the tomato purée evenly over the bottom. Top evenly with half of the tortilla strips and all of the corn. Spoon on another third of the purée, then top evenly with the remaining tortilla strips, all of the chiles, and all of the cheese. Top with the remaining sauce. Cover and bake for 30 minutes, until the sauce bubbles at the edges. Remove from the oven and allow to stand 5 minutes before serving.

Each serving provides:

275	Calories	48 g	Carbohydrate
11 g	Protein	221 mg	Sodium
6 g	Fat	10 mg	Cholesterol
8 g	Dietary Fiber		

Tamales and Other Masa Dishes

Corn is the age-old essence of Mexican cuisine and is enjoyed throughout the country in a variety of ways, most notably as masa—dough made from specially treated ground corn that is used to make tortillas, tamales, and other traditional specialties.

Tamales are standard fare at Mexican fiestas and holiday celebrations, and are always a wonderful treat. These succulent bundles of corn dough, filled with a tantalizing blend of savory or sweet ingredients, are among the most delicious of Mexican foods.

There seems to be a mystique surrounding the task of making tamales, perhaps because they are an ancient food, dating back at least four centuries. The simple truth of the matter, however, will be revealed after your first attempt. They are not at all difficult to prepare, but they are time-consuming, since a sauce and filling must be prepared, the dough must be mixed, and the masa bundles must be wrapped. But enlisting the help of loved ones makes quick work of these simple, enjoyable tasks.

Masa casseroles are an excellent, less elaborate way to enjoy corn dough, and are a great favorite of children and adults alike.

Tips and Tools

- The dough used for tamales is as important as the filling. Don't underwork the dough, and make sure it is moist and soft rather than crumbly, or it won't hold together.
- Dried corn husks are typically sold in 8-ounce packages. You will need no more than about a quarter of a package for 12 tamales. Select the largest ones for soaking so you don't have to piece together smaller ones.
- For an authentic touch, you may line the steamer rack with corn husks before placing the tamales on the rack.
- Banana leaves are available in the freezer case of many Mexican markets. Remove leaves from the package and thaw for a few hours before using. (See page 15 for more information about cooking tamales in banana leaves.)
- If you don't have a high-walled stockpot, you may cook the tamales in a large but shorter-walled pan. In this case, the tamales will be cooked lying flat, so you should fold the top flap down and tie the bundle closed with kitchen twine or long strips of corn husk. Place a metal steamer rack in the pot and add about 2 inches of water and a coin, which will rattle to warn you if the pan is going dry. Gently stack the tamales in an overlapping pattern. Arrange them so that they do not lie directly on top of

one another, or the ones on the bottom will be squashed. Cook as described in tamale recipes.

- With any of our tamale recipes, amounts can be multiplied to make additional tamales for freezing. Make and cook the tamales as directed, then place them in plastic bags to go into the freezer. There is no need to thaw frozen tamales before cooking—just steam them until heated through, about 15 to 20 minutes.

- Always serve tamales with a selection of salsas and condiments, such as salsa cruda, raw onion relish, and crema.

- A deep, large heavy-bottomed pot is required for steaming a dozen tamales at once. A metal or wooden steamer rack that fits inside the pot will hold the tamales up out of the water and prevent the dough from getting soggy.

- To spread or flatten masa for tamale pies, use the back of a wet spoon.

- Standard glass baking dishes are recommended for masa casseroles and tamale pies.

- Traditionally, diners open their own tamales and eat them directly from the wrappers.

Pumpkin Seed Tamales Filled with Eggs, Greens, and Tomatoes

This is most certainly not an authentic version of the Yucatecan tamales called Brazas de Reynas, *or Arms of the Queen, but it was inspired by that classic. The chaya leaves called for in the original are impossible to find—mustard greens make a reasonable substitute. We add ground pumpkin seeds and garlic-infused oil to the masa in place of the traditional lard to create a dough tasty enough to satisfy any aficionado of Mexican food. Hats off to Lynn Hager, old friend and chef extraordinaire, for taking good notes during her Mexican travels. Without her, this recipe would never have been born.*

Yield: 12 large tamales

Corn husks	12	**large***
The filling		
Eggs	6	**medium**
Mustard greens, chopped	4	**cups**
Fresh serrano chiles	3	**medium, minced**
Canola oil	1	**tablespoon**
White onion	1	**medium, finely diced**
Canned tomatoes, drained and chopped	3	**cups**
Garlic	3	**cloves, minced**
Salt	1½	**teaspoons**
Black pepper		**Several grinds**

*If you cannot find 12 large unbroken corn husks, overlap 2 smaller husks to make wrappers at least 6 inches wide and 7 inches long.

The dough

Raw unsalted pumpkin seeds	1	cup
Instant masa harina	4	cups
Salt	2	teaspoons
Mexican Vegetable Stock*	3	cups
Garlic Oil (page 36)	1	cup

Place the eggs in a stockpot with 6 cups of cold water and bring to a boil over high heat. When the water comes to a rolling boil, reduce the heat to medium-high and boil the eggs for 10 minutes. Immediately drain the eggs and transfer them to a bowl of ice water for 20 minutes. Peel the eggs and set them aside in a bowl.

Meanwhile, carefully wash the mustard greens, discarding the thickest part of the stems. Coarsely chop the leaves and set them aside. Remove and discard the stems of the chiles and scrape out the seeds and membranes for a milder filling. Finely mince the chiles. Heat the oil in a heavy-bottomed skillet over medium heat and sauté the onion until opaque, about 4 minutes. Add the tomatoes, chiles, garlic, salt, and pepper. Bring to a simmer over medium-high heat, then reduce heat to medium-low and cook 10 minutes. Stir in the chopped mustard greens and cook 2 more minutes. Transfer the sauce to a bowl and set aside.

Immerse the corn husks in a basin of hot water, weighting them down if necessary to keep them submerged, and soak for at least 30 minutes, until they are pliable. Pick over the husks carefully, discarding the corn silk and any other unwanted debris from each husk. Rinse them and shake them off, but don't carefully dry them. Set them aside on a plate or clean tea towel.

To make the dough, place the pumpkin seeds in a heavy-bottomed skillet over medium heat. Shake the pan frequently as they toast for a few minutes. When almost all the pumpkin seeds

*If you do not have Mexican Vegetable Stock on hand, make a batch according to the directions on page 38, or dissolve 1 large low-sodium vegetable broth cube in 3 cups of hot water.

have popped and are lightly browned, transfer them directly a food processor. Wait several minutes for the seeds to cool down a bit, then grind them to a fine powder and set them aside.

Combine the masa harina with the ground pumpkins seeds and salt in a large bowl. Add the stock and mix with your hands, working the dough until well-combined and soft. Add the garlic oil and work it in with your hands for a few minutes, until the dough is light and somewhat fluffy. Drop a pinch of dough into a glass of cold water to test its texture. If it floats, the dough is ready. If not, work it a bit longer and test again. When the dough is ready, cover the bowl with a damp tea towel until needed.

All the ingredients should be at room temperature when you assemble the tamales. Quarter each egg lengthwise and set the resulting wedges on a plate. Set up an assembly line, with corn husks, dough, eggs, and sauce close at hand. You will need a spoon for the sauce, a plate or clean board for each person who is wrapping tamales, and a large platter for the finished product.

Lay a large corn husk out on your work surface with the narrower end toward you. Divide the masa into 12 equal portions. Take 1 portion of dough and, with your fingers, spread it out directly on the husk to create a 4 × 4-inch layer of dough about ⅓ inch thick. Leave an unfilled border of about 1 inch on one side and at the top and bottom of the husk. On the remaining side, the dough can be spread all the way to the edge of the husk. Lay 2 egg wedges vertically along the center of the dough, then add about a twelfth of the sauce.

Pick up the side of the husk which has dough all the way to the edge and fold it over, wrapping the flap of unfilled husk over and around the outside of the tamale. This will enclose the filling completely inside the dough, and the entire tamale inside the husk. Fold the unfilled bottom husk up to seal in the bottom of the tamale. The top of each tamale can remain open.

As the tamales are finished, stack them on a platter. Place a metal steamer rack in a heavy-bottomed, high-walled stockpot and place about 2 inches of water in the pot, along with a clean coin, which will rattle to warn you if the pan is going dry.

Stand all the tamales up on the steamer rack, leaning them against the walls of the stockpot, open end at the top. It is fine for the tamales to rest against each other. You should be able to fit all the tamales in the pan at once.

Cover the pot and heat the water to boiling over high heat. When the pot begins to boil and steam—in about 10 minutes—reduce the heat to medium and maintain a steady simmer. Steam the tamales for 1 hour.

At some point during the cooking time, you will need to add more water to prevent the pan from going dry. Stay close to the pot so you will hear the coin when it rattles, or set your timer and check the pot every 15 minutes. Add very hot water, when needed, about 1 cup at a time, being careful not to pour it directly on top of the tamales.

Transfer the cooked tamales to a platter and serve hot.

Each tamal provides:

441	Calories	38 g	Carbohydrate
13 g	Protein	840 mg	Sodium
29 g	Fat	107 mg	Cholesterol
3 g	Dietary Fiber		

The Best 125 Meatless Mexican Dishes

Tamales Filled with Grilled Eggplant and Cheese

Here is another delicious lard-free masa dough, enhanced with garlic oil and chile powder. Excellent chile powder makes all the difference. Find a supplier of bulk herbs and spices—such as a natural food store—and taste different chile powders to find one that has a deep, complex flavor and no additives. Purchase chile powder in small quantities and check your home supply occasionally to make sure it is still flavorful; ground spices can lose their potency rather quickly.

Yield: 12 large tamales

Corn husks	12	**large**°
Ancho Chile Sauce		
Dried ancho chiles	3	large
Canned whole tomatoes	2	28-ounce cans, drained
Mexican Vegetable Stock°°	1¼	cups
White onion, coarsely chopped	1	medium
Fresh-squeezed lime juice	2	tablespoons
Dried Mexican oregano	1	tablespoon
Garlic	2	cloves
Brown sugar	1½	teaspoons
Salt	½	teaspoon

(continued)

°If you cannot find 12 large unbroken corn husks, overlap 2 smaller husks to make wrappers at least 6 inches wide and 7 inches long.

°If you do not have Mexican Vegetable Stock on hand, make a batch according to the directions on page 38, or dissolve 2 large low-sodium vegetable broth cubes in 3½ cups of hot water. This makes sufficient stock for both the sauce and the dough.

Ground allspice	¼	teaspoon
Black pepper		A few grinds
Canola oil	1	tablespoon
Fresh cilantro leaves, minced	⅓	cup

The filling

Eggplant	¾	pound (about 1 small)
White onions	2	small
Canola oil	2	teaspoons
Ancho Chile Sauce (see recipe above)	¾	cup
Mild feta cheese, crumbled	4	ounces (1 cup)
Garlic	1	clove, minced
Fresh cilantro leaves, minced	¼	cup

The dough

Instant masa harina	4	cups
Pure chile powder	2	tablespoons
Salt	2	teaspoons
Mexican Vegetable Stock	2¼	cups
Garlic Oil (page 36)	½	cup plus 2 tablespoons

Heat a griddle or cast-iron skillet over medium-high heat. Use your hands to tear the chiles into 3 or 4 pieces each, discarding the seeds and stems. Place the chile pieces in the hot pan and toast them for 1 to 2 minutes, occasionally pressing down on them with a metal spatula. Turn them over and briefly toast the other side. The chiles should blister and lighten in color.

When the chiles are toasted, place them in a food processor along with the tomatoes, stock, onion, lime juice, oregano, garlic, brown sugar, salt, allspice, and pepper. Purée until smooth.

Heat the oil in a heavy-bottomed skillet over medium heat. Stir the sauce into the hot oil and bring to a simmer. Cook, stirring frequently, 10 minutes. Stir in the cilantro and set the sauce aside.

To make the filling, preheat a coal or gas grill to medium-high, or preheat a broiler. Wash and dry the eggplant and trim off and discard the stem end. Without peeling the eggplant, cut it crosswise into ½-inch slices. Peel and trim the ends off the onions. Slice them crosswise into 1-inch slices. Lightly coat the cut sides of the eggplant and onion slices with the oil. Place the eggplant and onions on the hot grill and cook, turning frequently, until fairly soft and well charred, about 10 minutes. The onion will retain more of its texture than the eggplant. (Alternatively, you may prepare the vegetables by broiling them on both sides until soft and charred.) Transfer the vegetables to a plate to cool. When cool enough to handle, finely chop the eggplant and onions, including the charred portions. Combine with the ancho chile sauce, cheese, garlic, and cilantro and set aside.

Meanwhile, immerse the corn husks in a basin of hot water, weighting them down if necessary to keep them submerged, and soak for at least 30 minutes, until they are pliable. Pick over the husks carefully, discarding the corn silk and any other unwanted debris from each husk. Rinse them and shake them off, but don't carefully dry them. Set them aside on a plate or clean tea towel.

To make the dough, combine the masa harina with the chile powder and salt in a large bowl. Add the stock and mix with your hands, working the dough until well-combined and soft. Add the garlic oil and work it in with your hands for a few minutes, until the dough is light and somewhat fluffy. Drop a pinch of dough into a glass of cold water to test its texture. If it floats, the dough is ready. If not, work it a bit longer and test again. When the dough is ready, cover the bowl with a damp tea towel until needed.

(continued)

All ingredients should be at room temperature when you assemble the tamales. Set up an assembly line, with corn husks, dough, eggplant filling, and the cheese close at hand. You will need spoons for the eggplant and the cheese, a plate or clean board for each person who is wrapping tamales, and a large platter for the finished product.

Lay a large corn husk out on your work surface with the narrower end toward you. Divide the masa into 12 equal portions. Take 1 portion of dough and, with your fingers, spread it out directly on the husk to create a 4 × 4-inch layer of dough about ⅓ inch thick. Leave an unfilled border of about 1 inch on one side and at the top and bottom of the husk. On the remaining side, the dough can be spread all the way to the edge of the husk. Place about a twelfth of the eggplant filling down the center of the masa.

Pick up the side of the husk which has dough all the way to the edge and fold it over, wrapping the flap of unfilled husk over and around the outside of the tamale. This will enclose the filling completely inside the dough, and the entire tamale inside the husk. Fold the unfilled bottom husk up to seal in the bottom of the tamales. The top of each tamale can remain open.

As the tamales are finished, stack them on a platter. Place a metal steamer rack in a heavy-bottomed, high-walled stockpot and place about 2 inches of water in the pot, along with a clean coin, which will rattle to warn you if the pan is going dry. Stand all the tamales up on the steamer rack, leaning them against the walls of the stockpot, open end at the top. It is fine for the tamales to rest against each other. You should be able to fit all the tamales in the pan at once.

Cover the pot and heat the water to boiling over high heat. When the pot begins to boil and steam—in about 10 minutes— reduce the heat to medium and maintain a steady simmer. Steam the tamales for 1 hour.

At some point during the cooking time, you will need to add more water to prevent the pan from going dry. Stay close to the pot so you will hear the coin when it rattles, or set your timer and check the pot every 15 minutes. Add very hot water, when needed, about 1 cup at a time, being careful not to pour it directly on top of the tamales.

Just before the tamales are done, reheat the remaining Ancho Chile Sauce. Transfer the cooked tamales to a platter and serve hot with the sauce on the side.

Each tamal provides:

351	Calories	46 g	Carbohydrate
8 g	Protein	726 mg	Sodium
17 g	Fat	8 mg	Cholesterol
5 g	Dietary Fiber		

Tamales Filled with Roasted Corn, Black Beans, and Smoked Cheese

The smoky flavor of these tamales comes not just from the cheese, but from the roasted corn and tomatoes. The corn also contributes a sweetness and chewy texture to the filling. We think the rosemary-infused oil adds the crowning flavor note, but you may substitute Garlic Oil (page 36) or plain vegetable oil, if you wish.

Yield: 12 large tamales

Corn husks	12	**large**°
The filling		
Fresh corn	2	**medium ears**
Cooked black beans°°	1	**cup, drained**
Canned diced mild green chiles	1	**4-ounce can**
White onion, finely chopped	½	**medium**
Garlic	2	**cloves, minced**
Fresh rosemary leaves, minced	1	**teaspoon**
Salt	½	**teaspoon**
Black pepper		**Several grinds**
Smoked cheddar cheese, shredded	6	**ounces (1½ cups)**

°If you cannot find 12 large unbroken corn husks, overlap 2 smaller husks to make wrappers at least 6 inches wide and 7 inches long.

°°Cook dried beans according to the instructions on page 31, or purchase canned beans that do not contain additives.

The dough

Instant masa harina	4	**cups**
Salt	2	**teaspoons**
Mexican Vegetable Stock*	2¼	**cups**
Rosemary Oil (page 37)	½	**cup plus 2 tablespoons**

Immerse the corn husks in a basin of warm water, weighting them down if necessary to keep them submerged, and soak for at least 30 minutes, until they are pliable. Pick over the husks carefully, discarding corn silk and any other unwanted debris from each husk. Rinse them and shake them off, but don't carefully dry them. Set them aside on a plate or clean tea towel.

Preheat a coal or gas grill to high, or preheat the broiler. Remove the husks and silk from the corn. Grill or broil the corn about 10 minutes, turning a few times to expose all sides to the heat. Corn is done when slightly charred. Set the corn aside in a closed plastic bag for 10 minutes, then use a sharp knife to cut the charred corn kernels from the cob. In a bowl, combine the corn, beans, chiles, onion, garlic, rosemary, salt, pepper, and cheese. Set aside.

To make the dough, combine the masa harina with the salt in a large bowl. Add the stock and mix with your hands, working the dough until well combined and soft. Add the rosemary oil and work it in with your hands for a few minutes, until the dough is light and somewhat fluffy. Drop a pinch of dough into a glass of cold water to test its texture. If it floats, the dough is ready. If not, work it a bit longer and test again. When the dough is ready, cover the bowl with a damp tea towel until needed.

All the ingredients should be at room temperature when you assemble the tamales. Set up an assembly line, with corn husks, dough, and the filling close at hand. You will need a spoon

---

*If you do not have Mexican Vegetable Stock on hand, make a batch according to the directions on page 38, or dissolve 1 large low-sodium vegetable broth cube in 2¼ cups of hot water.

for the filling, a plate or clean board for each person who is wrapping tamales, and a large platter for the finished product.

Lay a large corn husk out on your work surface with the narrower end toward you. Divide the masa into 12 equal portions. Take 1 portion of dough and, with your fingers, spread it out directly on the husk to create a 4 × 4-inch layer of dough about ⅓ inch thick. Leave an unfilled border of about 1 inch on one side and at the top and bottom of the husk. On the remaining side the dough can be spread all the way to the edge of the husk. Place about a twelfth of the filling down the center of the masa.

Pick up the side of the husk which has dough all the way to the edge and fold it over, wrapping the flap of unfilled husk over and around the outside of the tamale. This will enclose the filling completely inside the dough, and the entire tamale inside the husk. Fold the unfilled bottom husk up to seal in the bottom of the tamales. The top of each tamale can remain open.

As the tamales are finished, stack them on a platter. Place a metal steamer rack in a heavy-bottomed, high-walled stockpot and place about 2 inches of water in the pot, along with a clean coin, which will rattle to warn you if the pan is going dry. Stand all the tamales up on the steamer rack, leaning them against the walls of the stockpot, open end at the top. It is fine for the tamales to rest against each other. You should be able to fit all the tamales in the pan at once.

Cover the pot and heat the water to boiling over high heat. When the pot begins to boil and steam—in about 10 minutes— reduce the heat to medium and maintain a steady simmer. Steam the tamales for 1 hour.

At some point during the cooking time, you will need to add more water to prevent the pan from going dry. Stay close to the pot so you will hear the coin when it rattles, or set your timer and check the pot every 15 minutes. Add very hot water, when needed, about 1 cup at a time, being careful not to pour it directly on top of the tamales.

Transfer the cooked tamales to a platter and serve hot.

Each tamal provides:

331	Calories	38 g	Carbohydrate
9 g	Protein	755 mg	Sodium
17 g	Fat	15 mg	Cholesterol
3 g	Dietary Fiber		

Masa Casserole with Corn, Zucchini, and Poblano Chiles

This is comfort food, Mexican-style. We love to serve colorful, flavorful casseroles, and find that diners of all ages enjoy them. If you cannot find panela cheese, substitute mozzarella.

Yield: 6 main-dish servings

Zucchini	2	medium (¾ pound)
Corn kernels, fresh or frozen*	3½	cups
Red bell pepper	1	medium, diced
Fresh poblano chiles	2	medium (⅓ pound)
Instant masa harina	1¼	cups
Salt	½	teaspoon
Garlic Oil (page 36)	1	tablespoon
Lowfat milk	1½	cups
Canola oil	¼	teaspoon
Eggs	4	large
Ground cumin	1	teaspoon
Pure chile powder	1	teaspoon
Ground cinnamon	½	teaspoon
Part-skim panela cheese, shredded	6	ounces (1½ cups)

*If you are using fresh corn, you will need about 7 medium ears to yield 3½ cups of kernels.

Grate the zucchini and put it in a bowl. Mix with the corn and bell pepper. Remove and discard the stem, seeds, and membranes from the chiles then finely mince them. Add to the corn mixture, stir to combine, and set aside.

Preheat the oven to 425 degrees F. In a medium saucepan, stir together the masa, salt, garlic oil, milk, and 1 cup of water. Heat over medium heat and cook for 5 to 7 minutes until thick, stirring frequently. Lightly oil an 8 × 8-inch or 2-quart casserole dish with the canola oil. Remove and reserve about 1 cup of the masa mixture, placing it in a covered dish. Pat the remaining masa on the bottom and 1 to 2 inches up the sides of the casserole dish. Place in the oven and bake for 10 minutes.

Meanwhile, beat the eggs with the cumin, chile powder, and cinnamon. Remove the partially baked masa from the oven and allow it to cool for several minutes. Evenly distribute the corn mixture on top of the masa. Sprinkle with the cheese then pour the egg mixture on top. Drop rounded tablespoonfuls of the reserved masa over the top, flattening slightly with the back of the spoon. Bake, uncovered, for 25 to 30 minutes, until the masa is slightly golden. Allow to sit for about 5 minutes before serving.

Each serving provides:

391	Calories	51 g	Carbohydrate
20 g	Protein	454 mg	Sodium
15 g	Fat	162 mg	Cholesterol
6 g	Dietary Fiber		

Masa and Black Bean Casserole

This bean and masa dish comes together quickly. It may be prepared in advance, and any leftovers may be heated in a warm oven to enjoy the next day. The slight heat from the chipotle chile is soothed by the crema and avocado.

Yield: 6 main-dish servings

Instant masa harina	1¼	**cups**
Salt	½	**teaspoon**
Lowfat milk	1½	**cups**
Garlic Oil (page 36)	2	**tablespoons**
Canola oil	¼	**teaspoon**
Carrots, diced	1	**cup**
Yellow onion, chopped	½	**cup**
Garlic	4	**cloves**
Cooked black beans*	2	**cups, drained**
Chipotle chiles en adobo, minced	1	**tablespoon**
Apple cider vinegar	2	**teaspoons**
Part-skim panela cheese	6	**ounces, sliced**
Ripe Haas avocado	1	**medium (½ pound)**
Lowfat Crema (page 34)	½	**cup**

Preheat the oven to 350 degrees F. In a medium saucepan, stir together the masa, salt, milk, 1 tablespoon of the garlic oil, and 1 cup of water. Heat over medium heat and cook for 5 to 7 minutes, until thick. Lightly oil an 8 × 8-inch or 2-quart casserole

---

*Cook dried beans according to the instructions on page 31, or purchase canned beans that do not contain additives.

dish with the canola oil. Remove and reserve about 1 cup of the masa mixture, placing it in a covered dish. Pat the remaining masa on the bottom and 1 to 2 inches up the sides of the casserole dish. Place in the oven and bake for 10 minutes. Meanwhile, put the diced carrots in a saucepan on a steamer rack and cook until just fork-tender, about 5 to 7 minutes. Remove from the heat and set aside. Place the remaining 1 tablespoon garlic oil in a skillet over medium heat. Add the onion and garlic and sauté for 3 to 4 minutes, until the onion is translucent. Place the beans, chile, and vinegar in a food processor. Add the sautéed onion and garlic. Purée until smooth.

Spoon half of the puréed bean mixture over the masa in the casserole dish. Top with the carrots and the cheese. Top with the remaining beans. Drop round tablespoons of the reserved masa over the top of the beans, flattening them slightly with the back of the spoon. Bake, uncovered, for 30 to 35 minutes, until the masa is slightly golden. Allow to sit for about 5 minutes before serving.

Cut the avocado open and remove the pit (see page 6). Peel the avocado and slice it. Serve the casserole, passing the avocado slices and crema.

━━ ━━━ ━━ ━━━ ━━ ━━━ ━ ━━━ ━

Each serving provides:

405	Calories	43 g	Carbohydrate
18 g	Protein	431 mg	Sodium
20 g	Fat	28 mg	Cholesterol
5 g	Dietary Fiber		

Sopes with Chorizo and Crema

These classic antojitos require some preparation time, but they are sure to launch a Mexican meal with authentic gusto. They also can be part of a lavish finger-food buffet—a fun and casual way to celebrate with friends. Simply multiply the recipe to serve more people. The tofu chorizo takes some advance planning. In fact, all the filling ingredients may be made well ahead of time, but the sopes should be cooked just a short time before serving. Their texture is best when still warm.

Yield: 12 sopes

The dough

Instant masa harina	2½	cups
Pure chile powder	2	teaspoons
Salt	1	teaspoon
Mexican Vegetable Stock*	1½	cups
Garlic Oil (page 36)	¼	cup
Canola oil for frying**		

The filling

Tofu Chorizo Sausage (page 40)	1½	cups
White onion, minced	½	cup
Green leaf lettuce, finely shredded	¾	cup
Mexican Crema (page 33)	¼	cup

*If you do not have Mexican Vegetable Stock on hand, make a batch according to the directions on page 38, or dissolve ½ large low-sodium vegetable broth cube in 1½ cups of hot water.

**Amount of oil needed will vary depending on the size of the pan used. Nutritional data includes 1½ tablespoons of oil, which is the amount absorbed by the sopes during frying.

In a mixing bowl, combine the masa harina with the chile powder and salt, then add the stock and garlic oil. Work the dough with your hands until well combined into a soft dough. If the dough is dry and crumbly, add lukewarm water, 1 tablespoon at a time, to correct the texture. If it is too wet and sticky, add additional masa harina, 1 tablespoon at a time. You want a dough that holds together well but does not stick very much to your hands.

Lay a clean tea towel out on your work surface. Form the dough into 12 balls about the size of a Ping-Pong ball. Roll each ball in your hands to achieve a smooth, round shape, then set the ball flat on the towel and press with your hand or a rolling pin to create a pancake shape an even ¼-inch thick.

Meanwhile, preheat a cast-iron griddle or heavy-bottomed skillet for at least 5 minutes over medium heat. Cook the dough cakes 5 to 6 minutes, turning them over after 3 minutes. Remove them from the hot pan to the work surface and allow to cool off for only about 1 minute, then use your fingers to pinch up a ridge all around the edge of the cake.

Set out the ingredients for the filling. Heat the canola oil in a heavy-bottomed skillet to a depth of ½-inch. When the oil is hot enough to sizzle a small bit of dough, place as many of the shaped sopes as will fit into the skillet without touching each other. Fry them for no more than 1 minute, then turn them over gently and fry for 30 seconds. Transfer to several layers of paper towels to drain off excess oil. Fill the sopes while hot.

Heap 2 tablespoons of chorizo onto each sope, then garnish with a portion of onion, lettuce, and a drizzling of crema. Serve the sopes as soon as possible.

Each sope provides:

199	Calories	23 g	Carbohydrate
5 g	Protein	293 mg	Sodium
11 g	Fat	7 mg	Cholesterol
2 g	Dietary Fiber		

Sopes with Black Beans and Tomatillo Salsa

VEGAN

Three popular Mexican flavors—those of black beans, radishes, and tomatillos—combine here to create a delicious and visually appetizing snack.

Yield: 12 sopes

The dough

Instant masa harina	2½ cups
Pure chile powder	2 teaspoons
Salt	1 teaspoon
Mexican Vegetable Stock*	1½ cups
Garlic Oil (page 36)	¼ cup
Canola oil for frying**	

The filling

Refried Black Beans (page 290)	1½ cups
Smooth Tomatillo Salsa (page 60)	¾ cup
Fresh red radishes	12 thin slices

In a mixing bowl, combine the masa harina with the chile powder and salt, then add the stock and garlic oil. Work the dough with your hands until well combined into a soft dough. If the

---

*If you do not have Mexican Vegetable Stock on hand, make a batch according to the directions on page 38, or dissolve ½ large low-sodium vegetable broth cube in 1½ cups of hot water.

**Amount of oil needed will vary, depending on the size of the pan used. Nutritional data includes 1½ tablespoons of oil, which is the amount absorbed by the sopes during frying.

dough is dry and crumbly, add lukewarm water, 1 tablespoon at a time, to correct the texture. If it is too wet and sticky, add additional masa harina, 1 tablespoon at a time. You want a dough that holds together well but does not stick very much to your hands.

Lay a clean tea towel out on your work surface. Form the dough into 12 balls about the size of a Ping-Pong ball. Roll each ball in your hands to achieve a smooth, round shape, then set the ball flat on the towel and press with your hand or a rolling pin to create a pancake shape an even ¼-inch thick.

Meanwhile, preheat a cast-iron griddle or heavy-bottomed skillet for at least 5 minutes over medium heat. Cook the dough cakes 5 to 6 minutes, turning them over after 3 minutes. Remove them from the hot pan to the work surface and allow to cool off for only about 1 minute, then use your fingers to pinch up a ridge all around the edge of the cake.

Set out the ingredients for the filling. Heat the canola oil in a heavy-bottomed skillet to a depth of ½ inch. When the oil is hot enough to sizzle a small bit of dough, place as many of the shaped sopes as will fit into the pan without touching each other. Fry them for no more than 1 minute, then turn them over gently and fry for 30 seconds. Transfer to several layers of paper towels to drain off excess oil. Fill the sopes while hot.

Heap 2 tablespoons of beans onto each sope, then garnish with a portion of tomatillo salsa and top with a slice of radish. Serve the sopes as soon as possible.

━ ━━ ━ ━━ ━ ━━ ━ ━━ ━

Each sope provides:

181	Calories	25 g	Carbohydrate
4 g	Protein	214 mg	Sodium
8 g	Fat	0 mg	Cholesterol
2 g	Dietary Fiber		

Gorditas Stuffed with Refried Beans

VEGAN

Gorditas (literally, little fat ones) are like thick, stuffed tortillas and
are a great way to use up leftover refried beans. There many variations on the gordita theme; each region or even family may have
its own traditional recipe. This recipe makes gorditas that are a
mouthwatering treat for lunch or as an appetizer. Let each diner
garnish their own with shredded green leaf lettuce and Salsa Cruda
(page 54) or your favorite red table sauce.

Yield: 8 gorditas

Masa harina	**1½ cups**
Salt	**¼ teaspoon**
Garlic Oil (page 36)	**1 tablespoon**
Refried Black Beans	
(page 290)	**¼ cup**
Canola oil for frying*	

Combine the masa harina with the salt, then add 1 cup water
and the garlic oil and work for a few minutes with your hands
to create a smooth, soft dough. Work in more water, 1 tablespoon at a time, if the dough is crumbly rather than soft.
Divide the dough into 12 equal balls. Pick up a ball and make a
deep indentation in the center with your thumb. Place about
1 teaspoon of the beans into the indentation and pinch the
dough closed over them. With your hands, pat the ball into a
½-inch-thick circle. It is fine if the beans bleed through the
dough. Form 12 patties in this manner and set them aside on
a plate.

---

*Amount of oil needed will vary, depending on the size of pan used. Nutri-
tional data includes 2 tablespoons of oil, which is the amount absorbed by the
gorditas during frying.

Meanwhile, pour the canola oil into a heavy-bottomed skillet to a depth of ¼-inch and heat it over medium heat until hot enough to sizzle a speck of masa. When the oil is hot enough, place a few gorditas in the pan and fry 3 to 4 minutes per side, until lightly browned. Drain briefly on layers of paper towels and serve immediately with your garnishes of choice on the side. Do not allow the gorditas to cool off too much before serving; their texture is best when freshly cooked and piping hot.

━ ━━━ ━━ ━━━ ━━ ━━━ ━ ━━━ ━

Each gordita provides:

131	Calories	18 g	Carbohydrate
2 g	Protein	68 mg	Sodium
6 g	Fat	0 mg	Cholesterol
1 g	Dietary Fiber		

Egg Dishes

In a meatless diet, eggs are one of the most cholesterol-rich foods, so we don't eat them every day. On occasion, though, when a quick protein boost is desired, eggs can be satisfying, tasty nourishment.

The people of Mexico enjoy eggs immensely, and many village households keep chickens for an always-fresh supply. Traditionally, the main meal of the day is a hearty mid-afternoon *comida,* and egg dishes might be served late in the evening as a light supper entrée. They also may appear, as they do typically in the rest of North America, as a breakfast or late morning brunch.

Most of the dishes in this chapter are suitable for either morning or evening meals. In addition, the pickled eggs are a marvelous snack, and the baked omelets could be served as appetizers, cut into appropriately small servings.

We invite you to enjoy the versatility of eggs in the Mexican style.

Tips and Tools

- We prefer to purchase eggs from free-range or "run-around" hens that have not been raised under crowded conditions. Antibiotics and hormones are routinely fed to most commercially raised hens, and some researchers warn that the meat and eggs of these birds can pose health risks. Look for eggs from free-range, natural-diet hens. If you don't find them at your local market, ask the grocer to look for a source for these more "natural" eggs.

- Except for the pickled eggs and those dishes requiring poached eggs, our recipes can be made using egg substitutes when cholesterol is a concern. They come in frozen, refrigerated, or powdered form. You may wish to sample various types, following the instructions on the packages.

- Don't overwhip eggs before scrambling them. Their texture will be most appetizing if they are gently stirred just enough to mix the yolks into the whites.

- A seasoned cast-iron skillet is our preferred cookware for stove-top egg dishes. The baked omelets require standard glass baking dishes.

Pickled Eggs with Mexican Spices

*Pickled eggs are a little-known treat in the U.S. outside of brew pubs.
But a half or whole pickled egg is a delicious addition when serving
a simple lunch or presenting a selection of appetizers. This recipe
is a yummy variation on the standard theme. Of course, the spiciness
from the pickled jalapeño chiles will be prized by our heat-
seeking friends.*

Yield: 12 pickled eggs

Eggs	12	**large**
Garlic	10	**cloves, peeled**
Bay leaves	4	
Fresh cilantro	6	**leafy sprigs**
Fresh jalapeño chiles	2	**quartered lengthwise**
Allspice berries	6,	**crushed**
Dried marjoram	½	**teaspoon**
Apple cider vinegar	1½	**cups**
Fresh-squeezed lime juice	¼	**cup**
Salt	1	**teaspoon**

Place the eggs in a stockpot with 12 cups of cold water and bring
to a rolling boil over high heat.

When a rolling boil has been achieved, reduce the heat to
medium-high and cook 10 minutes. Immediately drain the eggs
and transfer them to a bowl of ice water for 20 minutes. Peel the
eggs and pack them into two quart jars, 6 eggs to a jar. Distribute the garlic, bay leaves, cilantro sprigs, chiles, allspice berries,
and marjoram equally between the two jars.

Combine the vinegar and lime juice with 1½ cup of cool water and dissolve the salt in this liquid. Pour over the contents of the jars, leaving at least 1 inch of headroom. Cover the jars and store in the refrigerator for at least a few days or up to 2 weeks before serving.

Each egg provides:

78	Calories	1 g	Carbohydrate
6 g	Protein	151 mg	Sodium
5 g	Fat	213 mg	Cholesterol
0 g	Dietary Fiber		

Nopalitos with Zucchini, Tomatoes, and Eggs

This dish is delicious for breakfast or as a light dinner. Serve it with corn tortillas—blue corn tortillas are particularly pretty.

Yield: 4 main-dish servings

Fresh nopales	¼	pound
Fresh serrano chiles	3	medium
Fresh pear tomatoes	½	pound
Zucchini	1	medium (about ⅓ pound)
Yellow bell pepper	1	medium
Olive oil	1	tablespoon
Dark rum	1	tablespoon
Garlic	2	cloves, minced
Salt	½	teaspoon
Fresh cilantro leaves, minced	¼	cup
Eggs	2	large

The thorns of the nopales, which are lodged under the small bumps that irregularly dot the paddles, usually have been shaved off by the grower. If not, use the dull edge of a knife blade to scrape off the thorns, taking care not to stick yourself. Do not remove the peel, however. Lay the nopales flat on your work surface and cut off and discard ¼-inch of the outer rim and the base end. Slice the paddles lengthwise into ¼-inch strips, then cut the strips into 1-inch pieces. Place the cactus strips in a saucepan and cover with water. Bring to a boil, reduce the heat to medium-high, cover the pan, and cook for about 15 minutes, until fork-tender. (The cooking time may vary depending on the freshness of the cactus.) Drain into a colander and rinse well with cold water. Pat dry with a tea towel and set aside.

Remove and discard the stems of the chiles and scrape out the seeds for a milder dish. Finely mince the chiles and set them aside. Cut out and discard the stem ends of the tomatoes and, without peeling, dice them and set aside in a bowl. Dice the zucchini. Discard the stem, seeds, and white membranes of the bell pepper and dice it.

Heat the oil and rum over medium heat in a large heavy-bottomed skillet, add the garlic, and sauté for about 1 minute. Stir in the cactus, tomatoes, zucchini, bell pepper, and salt. Cook for 15 minutes, stirring occasionally. Add the cilantro and continue to cook for about 5 minutes.

Meanwhile, crack the eggs into a small bowl and gently stir them together to combine the yolks with the whites. Pour into the skillet and stir to incorporate. Cook and stir for 1 to 2 minutes until the eggs have set. Serve immediately.

Each serving provides:

115	Calories	11 g	Carbohydrate
5 g	Protein	311 mg	Sodium
6 g	Fat	107 mg	Cholesterol
3 g	Dietary Fiber		

Scrambled Eggs with Tomatillos and Potatoes

We prefer to make this breakfast or dinner entrée with yellow Finn or white rose potatoes, but any thin-skinned new potato would work well, such as the standard red variety. We recommend serving this dish with warm tortillas and salsa or Guacamole (page 88) and chips.

Yield: 4 main-dish servings

Fresh tomatillos	¼	**pound (3 medium)**
Salt	¼	**teaspoon**
Pure chile powder	½	**teaspoon**
Ground cumin	¼	**teaspoon**
Yellow Finn potatoes	1	**pound**
Canola oil	2	**tablespoons**
Yellow onion	½	**medium, chopped**
Fresh rosemary, minced	1	**tablespoon**
Canned diced mild green chiles	2	**tablespoons**
Eggs	4	**medium**
Part-skim queso fresco, crumbled	2	**ounces (½ cup)**

Remove and discard the husks of the tomatillos. Rinse the tomatillos and place them in a saucepan along with the salt. Cover with water, bring to a boil, reduce the heat to medium-high, and simmer about 10 minutes, until they are very tender. Drain and place the tomatillos in a food processor along with the chile powder and cumin and pulse to chop. Set aside.

Meanwhile, scrub the potatoes and cut them into bite-size cubes. Place them in a pan and cover with water. Bring to a boil over high heat, reduce the heat to medium, and cook 8 to 10 minutes, until barely fork-tender, but not falling apart. Drain well.

Heat the oil in a large heavy-bottomed skillet over medium-high heat. Add the onion and rosemary and sauté for about 2 minutes, until the onion is limp, stirring occasionally. Add the potatoes and continue to cook for about 10 minutes until the potatoes begin to brown. Toss frequently during the cooking time.

Stir in the tomatillos and chiles, and continue to cook for about 3 minutes. (The pan will sizzle when you add them.) Meanwhile, crack the eggs into a bowl and gently stir them together to combine the yolks and whites. Add them to the skillet and stir almost constantly for about 5 minutes, until the eggs are set. Turn off the heat and sprinkle the cheese over the top. Cover the pan and allow the cheese to melt for about 1 minute. Serve immediately.

Each serving provides:

296	Calories	27 g	Carbohydrate
12 g	Protein	353 mg	Sodium
16 g	Fat	221 mg	Cholesterol
5 g	Dietary Fiber		

Scrambled Eggs with Green Beans and Tomatoes

ALMOST INSTANT

In Mexico, lunch is the main meal of the day and egg dishes often appear at the evening meal. Whether you make this recipe for breakfast, brunch, lunch, or dinner, this combination is a winner. Of course, you may simply multiply the recipe if you are cooking for more than two people.

Yield: 2 main-dish servings

Fresh green beans	¼	**pound**
Unsalted butter	1	**tablespoon**
Green onions	3	**medium, minced**
Tomatoes, fresh or canned, chopped	½	**cup**
Pure chile powder	½	**teaspoon**
Salt	¼	**teaspoon**
Black pepper		**A few grinds**
Eggs	4	**large**
Dried Mexican oregano	½	**teaspoon**

Rinse the green beans, remove the stems ends, and pull off strings, if necessary. Chop the beans into roughly 1-inch pieces. Steam or parboil the beans until barely fork-tender, about 8 minutes. Rinse briefly with cold water, drain, and set aside.

Meanwhile, in a small skillet, melt the butter and sauté the green onions with the tomatoes, chile powder, salt, and pepper for 5 minutes. In a small bowl, gently stir the eggs together to combine the yolks and whites. Add the eggs and green beans to the skillet and stir and cook until the eggs are set to your liking, about 5 minutes. Transfer to two warmed serving plates and sprinkle each serving with ¼ teaspoon of the oregano. Serve hot.

Each serving provides:

245	Calories	10 g	Carbohydrate
15 g	Protein	161 mg	Sodium
17 g	Fat	443 mg	Cholesterol
2 g	Dietary Fiber		

Huevos Rancheros

This version of a classic dish poaches the eggs in a chunky, well seasoned tomato sauce. We enjoy it for brunch, and on occasion for a simple dinner. Some of your diners may enjoy more than 1 egg, so feel free to poach additional eggs in the sauce, or on the side.

Yield: 8 main-dish servings

Dried ancho chiles	2	**medium**
Olive oil	1	**tablespoon**
Yellow onion	1	**medium, diced**
Garlic	4	**cloves, minced**
Ground cumin	½	**teaspoon**
Ground coriander	½	**teaspoon**
Salt	½	**teaspoon**
Ready-cut tomatoes	2	**28-ounce cans**
Corn tortillas	8	**standard-size**
Eggs	8	**large**
Part-skim queso fresco, crumbled	1	**ounce (¼ cup)**
Fresh cilantro leaves, minced	2	**tablespoons**

Tear the ancho chiles open and discard the stems and seeds. Use kitchen scissors or a sharp knife to sliver the chiles. Heat the olive oil over medium heat in a large heavy-bottomed skillet and add the onion. Sauté for 3 to 4 minutes, until the onion begins to soften. Add the garlic, chiles, cumin, coriander, and salt. Cook for about 1 minute, stirring constantly, then add the tomatoes along with their juice, increase the heat to medium-high, and bring the sauce to a simmer. Simmer, stirring frequently, about 30 minutes to reduce the sauce.

Shortly before the sauce is finished, warm the tortillas (see page 30) and wrap them in a clean tea towel to keep them warm.

Gently break the eggs into the finished sauce, cover the pan, and cook for 5 to 7 minutes, until the whites of the eggs are completely set. Place a warm tortilla on each plate. Gently scoop out an egg, along with some of the sauce, and place on top of each tortilla. Equally distribute the remaining sauce over each portion, then top with cheese and cilantro. Serve immediately.

Each serving provides:

233	Calories	29 g	Carbohydrate
11 g	Protein	311 mg	Sodium
8 g	Fat	215 mg	Cholesterol
3 g	Dietary Fiber		

Eggs Poached in Garlic Tomato Sauce with Chile Strips and Cheese

ALMOST INSTANT

Here is a delicious brunch entrée to impress your friends, or a lunch or supper main course for the family. Serve the eggs with Cornbread with Whole Kernels (page 98) or warm tortillas, and include a bean side dish and a hearty vegetable salad for an evening meal.

Yield: 4 main-dish servings

Canned whole mild green chiles	2	
Mexican Vegetable Stock*	1½	**cups**
Canned tomatoes, drained and chopped	⅔	**cup**
Garlic	2	**cloves**
Olive oil	1	**teaspoon**
Apple cider vinegar	1	**teaspoon**
Salt	¼	**teaspoon**
Granulated sugar	¼	**teaspoon**
Eggs	4	**large**
Mild feta cheese, crumbled	1	**ounce (¼ cup)**

Cut the chiles lengthwise into ¼-inch strips, then cut the strips into 1-inch lengths. Set aside. Combine the stock, tomatoes, garlic, olive oil, vinegar, salt, and sugar in a blender and purée until smooth. Pour into a medium heavy-bottomed skillet and bring to a brisk simmer over medium heat. Simmer, stirring occasionally, until reduced by about one-third, about 10 minutes.

*If you do not have Mexican Vegetable Stock on hand, make a batch according to the directions on page 38, or dissolve ½ large low-sodium vegetable broth cube in 1½ cups of hot water.

Gently break the eggs into the reduced sauce. Poach the eggs about 5 to 7 minutes, ladling the bubbling sauce over them. The eggs are done when the whites are completely set.

Serve the hot eggs along with the sauce, 1 egg to a serving, in shallow bowls. Top each serving with 1 tablespoon of cheese and a portion of the chile strips.

Each serving provides:

121	Calories	5 g	Carbohydrate
8 g	Protein	525 mg	Sodium
8 g	Fat	219 mg	Cholesterol
0 g	Dietary Fiber		

Baked Green Chile and Cheese Omelet

We enjoy this easy-to-prepare dish for breakfast or cut into small squares for an evening appetizer. Serve with salsa, sour cream, and tortillas, if you wish.

Yield: 6 side-dish servings

Canola oil	¼	teaspoon
Canned whole mild green chiles	1	4-ounce can
Eggs	5	medium
Part-skim panela cheese, shredded	6	ounces (1½ cups)
Lowfat milk	2	tablespoons
Yellow onion, minced	¼	cup
Garlic	1	clove, minced
Salt	¼	teaspoon
Dried Mexican oregano	½	teaspoon
Pure chile powder	¼	teaspoon
Ground cumin	¼	teaspoon
Ground coriander	¼	teaspoon

Preheat the oven to 325 degrees F. Lightly oil a 2-quart casserole dish with the canola oil. Drain the whole chiles and arrange them on the bottom of the casserole. In a blender, combine the eggs, cheese, milk, onion, garlic, salt, oregano, chile powder, cumin, and coriander. Mix at low speed for about 1 minute, then evenly pour the mixture over the chiles. Bake, uncovered, 30 minutes. Let cool about 5 minutes before serving.

Each serving provides:

153	Calories	3 g	Carbohydrate
13 g	Protein	488 mg	Sodium
11 g	Fat	192 mg	Cholesterol
0 g	Dietary Fiber		

Baked Tortilla Omelet with Spinach, Cilantro, and Green Chiles

This baked egg dish is full of flavor, but not too spicy hot. Serve a shot of tequila on the rocks as the accompanying beverage if you have adventuresome guests.

Yield: 6 main-dish servings

Fresh spinach	¾	pound (about 1 bunch)
Canola oil	1	tablespoon plus ¼ teaspoon
Yellow onion	1	small, diced
Garlic	2	cloves, minced
Fresh cilantro leaves	1	cup, loosely packed
Canned diced mild green chiles	1	4-ounce can
Black olives, chopped	2	tablespoons
Slightly stale corn tortillas	4	standard-size
Eggs	4	large
Egg whites	2	large
Nonfat dry milk	2	tablespoons
Ground cumin	½	teaspoon
Pure chile powder	½	teaspoon
Lowfat Crema (page 34)	¼	cup
Jack cheese, shredded	2	ounces (½ cup)

Preheat the oven to 350 degrees F. Carefully wash the spinach, discarding the stems. Set spinach leaves aside in a colander to drain. Heat the 1 tablespoon oil in a large heavy-bottomed skillet and add the onion and garlic. Sauté for about 1 minute, then add the spinach and cilantro. Cover and steam over medium-low heat for 5 minutes. Turn off the heat and stir in the chiles and olives. Set aside.

Slice the tortillas all the way across into strips about 1 inch wide. Whisk together the eggs, egg whites, and dry milk. Add the cumin and chile powder, then whisk in the crema. Oil a deep-dish pie pan with the ¼ teaspoon oil and spoon the spinach mixture evenly over the bottom. Top evenly with the tortilla strips and then with the cheese. Pour the egg mixture evenly over the top, tipping the pan slightly to distribute it through the tortillas. Bake, uncovered, for 25 to 30 minutes, until eggs are set. Allow to cool for 5 minutes before serving. Serve hot, or at room temperature.

Each serving provides:

210	Calories	17 g	Carbohydrate
12 g	Protein	395 mg	Sodium
11 g	Fat	156 mg	Cholesterol
3 g	Dietary Fiber		

Baked Tortilla Omelet with Zucchini and Mushrooms

This dish is delicious hot from the oven, but also wonderful at room temperature. You also can hold it in the refrigerator to enjoy a day later. The marjoram and sherry vinegar impart a unique flavor.

Yield: 6 main-dish servings

Zucchini	3	**medium (about 1 pound)**
Button mushrooms	½	**pound**
Fresh serrano chiles	2	**medium**
Canola oil	1	**tablespoon plus ¼ teaspoon**
Dried marjoram	1	**teaspoon**
Salt	¼	**teaspoon**
Black pepper		**Several grinds**
Sherry vinegar	2	**tablespoons**
Slightly stale corn tortillas	3	**standard-size**
Eggs	4	**large**
Egg whites	2	**large**
Nonfat dry milk	2	**tablespoons**
Mild feta cheese, crumbled	2	**ounces (½ cup)**

Remove the stem ends from the zucchini and cut the zucchini into ¼-inch rounds. Brush or wipe the dirt from the mushrooms and thinly slice them. Remove and discard the stems of the chiles and scrape out the seeds for a milder dish. Finely mince the chiles.

Heat the 1 tablespoon oil in a large heavy-bottomed skillet over medium heat. Add the zucchini, chiles, marjoram, salt, and pepper. Sauté for 8 to 10 minutes, stirring occasionally, until the zucchini is just fork-tender and beginning to brown. Add the mushrooms to the skillet along with the sherry vinegar. Continue to cook for about 10 minutes, stirring frequently. The mushrooms will begin to brown slightly.

Meanwhile, preheat the oven to 350 degrees F. Cut the tortillas into strips about 1 inch wide. Whisk together the eggs, egg whites, and dry milk. Lightly oil a deep-dish pie pan with the ¼ teaspoon oil. Distribute half of the sautéed vegetables evenly over the bottom of the pan. Cover with the tortilla strips. Evenly distribute the cheese, then the remaining half of the vegetables over the tortilla strips. Pour the egg mixture evenly over the casserole and bake, uncovered, 20 minutes. Turn on the broiler and continue to bake for 5 minutes to slightly crisp the top and finish cooking the eggs. Allow to cool for 5 minutes before slicing. Serve hot, or at room temperature.

Each serving provides:

183	Calories	17 g	Carbohydrate
10 g	Protein	311 mg	Sodium
9 g	Fat	151 mg	Cholesterol
3 g	Dietary Fiber		

Stuffed Chiles with Savory Cocoa Mole

An exotic masterpiece, this classic mole *combines cocoa, cinnamon, and cloves with tomatoes for a dense, rich, mysterious flavor. Serve this version of chiles rellenos with Red Rice with Peas (page 258), Refried Black Beans (page 290), and flour tortillas for a delicious meal. We use the traditional queso fresco available in Mexican markets; if you are unable to locate it, substitute farmer cheese. Poblano chiles are the perfect choice for stuffing, though any long, mild green chile, such as the Anaheim, could be substituted.*

Yield: 8 main-dish servings

Fresh poblano chiles	8	large (about 1½ pounds)
Peeled and crushed pear tomatoes	1	28-ounce can
Yellow onion	½	medium, chopped
Garlic	3	cloves, minced
Unsweetened powdered cocoa	2	teaspoons
Ground cinnamon	½	teaspoon
Pure chile powder	½	teaspoon
Ground cumin	½	teaspoon
Dry mustard		Scant ⅛ teaspoon
Ground cloves		Scant ⅛ teaspoon
Part-skim queso fresco, crumbled	10	ounces (2½ cups)

Egg whites	3	large
Egg	1	large
Unbleached flour	1	tablespoon
Fine dry bread crumbs	1	tablespoon
Canola oil	2	tablespoons

Roast the chiles on a hot grill or under a broiler for about 5 minutes, or until the skin is uniformly charred. Turn and blacken the other side, being careful not to tear the chiles. Carefully lay them on a glass platter and cover with plastic wrap. Set aside at room temperature for about 15 minutes; the steam inside the wrapping will finish cooking the chiles.

Meanwhile, place the tomatoes, onion, and garlic in a blender or food processor and purée until smooth. Pour into a large heavy-bottomed skillet and add the cocoa, cinnamon, chile powder, cumin, mustard, and cloves. Cook over medium heat, stirring frequently, 8 to 10 minutes, until thickened. Set aside.

When the chiles are cool enough to handle, gently remove the skins. Carefully make a slit lengthwise through only one side of each chili, starting ½ inch from the stem end. Use a spoon to carefully scrape out and discard the seeds and membranes, but be careful not to detach the stems from the chiles.

Stuff the chiles with equal portions of cheese, compacting the cheese in your hands to conform to the shape of the chiles. Overlap the slit edges of the chiles slightly as you finish filling them, and set aside.

Separate the yolk from the white of the whole egg, and beat all 4 egg whites until they are stiff, but not dry. Add the egg yolk and beat to incorporate. Add the flour and bread crumbs, then beat again to incorporate. Pour the batter onto a large platter, or into a pie pan.

(continued)

Heat 1 tablespoon of the oil in a large cast-iron skillet over medium-high heat. (The skillet should be large enough to hold 4 chiles at a time.) Carefully dip 4 of the filled chiles in the batter, 1 at a time, to generously coat them, and gently place them in the hot skillet. Fry the stuffed chiles 4 to 5 minutes, until golden brown, then turn and cook 4 to 5 minutes on the other side.

Meanwhile, reheat the sauce and pour it into a large, shallow baking dish. Slide the cooked chiles into the sauce and hold them in a warm oven. Repeat the cooking process with the remaining 4 chiles. When all the chiles are cooked and immersed in the sauce, serve immediately, or keep warm in the oven until ready to serve.

Each serving provides:

207	Calories	14 g	Carbohydrate
12 g	Protein	274 mg	Sodium
12 g	Fat	46 mg	Cholesterol
2 g	Dietary Fiber		

Chorizo and Scrambled Eggs

ALMOST INSTANT

In Mexico, this dish might be served for supper, along with salsa fresca, beans, and warm corn tortillas. Of course, it also makes a wonderful breakfast or brunch entrée. Simply multiply the recipe to serve more than two people. The vegetarian chorizo can be prepared up to a few days ahead of time.

Yield: 2 main-dish servings

Canola oil	2	**teaspoons**
White onion, minced	¼	**cup**
Eggs	3	**large**
Salt		**A pinch**
Tofu Chorizo Sausage		
(page 40)	½	**cup**
Fresh cilantro leaves, minced	2	**tablespoons**

Heat the oil over medium heat in a small well-seasoned cast-iron skillet. Add the onion and sauté for 5 minutes, stirring frequently. Meanwhile, gently stir the eggs together, along with the salt, to combine the yolks with the whites. When the onion is softened, add the eggs and chorizo to the skillet and cook, stirring and turning constantly, until the eggs are set to your liking, about 5 minutes. Sprinkle with cilantro. Serve hot.

■ ▬▬ ■ ▬▬ ■ ▬▬ ■ ▬▬ ■

Each serving provides:

226	Calories	7 g	Carbohydrate
13 g	Protein	295 mg	Sodium
16 g	Fat	320 mg	Cholesterol
1 g	Dietary Fiber		

Rice and Pasta Dishes

Neither rice nor pasta is indigenous to Mexico, but both have their place in its traditional cuisines. Rice, in particular, is a staple, appearing frequently as a side dish, along with the ubiquitous bean. Rather than choose just one or two favorites, we have included several side-dish rice variations in this chapter. All are versatile, distinctive, and delicious.

Though long-grain white rice is traditional in Mexico, most of our recipes are suitable for either brown or white rice. Avoid converted rice, however; its texture is unsuited to these dishes.

Pasta, a relatively recent import from Italy, is hearty and economical and has been embraced warmly in some parts of

Mexico. A favorite pasta shape is coiled vermicelli, or *fideo,* which is typically browned, then cooked in soups or baked with sauce. Our pasta recipes, for the most part, could not be considered traditional, but combine the seasonings of Mexico with vegetables and pasta in creative ways.

Tips and Tools for Rice

- Because long-grain white rice is the rice of choice in Mexico, we have called for it in our rice dishes. However, if you prefer, most of them can be made with good but different results using long-grain brown rice, which will lend a chewier texture to the finished dish. If you choose to substitute brown rice in these recipes, increase the cooking time to 45 to 50 minutes.
- Cook rice in a heavy-bottomed pan with a tight-fitting lid—enameled cast-iron is perfect.

Tips and Tools for Pasta

- The most important tip for cooking pasta is to use a large pot containing several quarts of water so the pasta can move around easily. Bring the water to a full rolling boil before adding the pasta, and vigorously stir the pasta occasionally during the cooking time. A long-handled wooden spoon is ideal for stirring pasta.
- Some cooks consider it essential to add oil and salt to pasta cooking water, but we achieve excellent results without adding either.
- Our recipes suggest cooking pasta to the al dente stage. This Italian phrase (literally, to the tooth) suggests that the tooth should meet a little resistance when biting into

the pasta. Undercooked pasta has a tough center and an unpleasant starchy taste; overcooked, it falls apart easily and has a mushy texture.

- Drain pasta in a large footed colander. Don't rinse cooked pasta unless it is to be used for a cold salad.

Pumpkin Ravioli with Creamy Jalapeño Rosemary Sauce

Although traditional Mexican cuisine does not specialize in stuffed pasta dishes, these ravioli include native flavorings. To enjoy these homemade ravioli with a no-fuss preparation, we take an unconventional shortcut and use wonton wrappers. You may prepare your favorite pasta dough recipe, if you prefer. For a milder dish, you may remove the seeds of the pickled jalapeños. This dish is a wonderful autumn treat!

Yield: 8 main-dish servings

The ravioli

Wonton wrappers	1	12-ounce package
Raw unsalted pumpkin seeds	2	tablespoons
Pumpkin purée	1	16-ounce can
Garlic	2	cloves, minced
Fresh rosemary, minced	1	teaspoon
Salt	¼	teaspoon
Black pepper	⅛	teaspoon

The sauce

Unsalted butter	2	tablespoons
Garlic	2	cloves, minced
Fresh rosemary, minced	1	teaspoon
Unbleached flour	2	tablespoons
Lowfat milk	1½	cups
Pickled jalapeño chiles, minced	2	teaspoons

Bring the wonton wrappers to room temperature. Place the pumpkin seeds in a single layer in a heavy-bottomed skillet over medium-high heat. Shake the pan frequently. Soon the nuts will begin to pop and turn golden brown, emitting a wonderful roasted aroma. Remove immediately from the skillet and set aside. When cool enough to handle, chop them.

Combine the pumpkin purée, 2 cloves garlic, 1 teaspoon minced rosemary, the salt, and pepper. Enlist a helper to assist in filling the ravioli. Have the wrappers, the filling, the chopped pumpkin seeds, and a small bowl of water close at hand. Lay a wrapper flat on a plate or the countertop and use your fingers to moisten all around the edges of the dough with water. Place a rounded teaspoon of the filling in the center of the wrapper, sprinkle on a few toasted pumpkin seeds and top with another wonton wrapper. Pinch the edges together to seal tightly, pressing out any trapped air as you go. Press around the sealed edges with the tines of a fork. As you finish them, wrap the filled ravioli in a lightly floured tea towel so they do not dry out. Allow to stand at room temperature for 30 minutes to 1 hour.

In a stockpot, bring several quarts of water to a rapid boil. Meanwhile, begin to prepare the sauce. Melt the butter in a heavy-bottomed skillet over medium heat. Stir in 2 cloves garlic and 1 teaspoon rosemary and cook for about 2 minutes. Whisk in the flour and continue to cook for about 1 minute, whisking constantly. Gradually whisk in the milk and continue to cook for about 6 minutes, until slightly thickened. Stir the chiles into the sauce. Turn the heat down to very low, and stir the sauce frequently to prevent scorching.

While the sauce is thickening, gently drop half of the raviolis into the boiling water and cook for about 4 minutes, until the wonton wrappers turn from opaque to translucent and are tender. Remove the cooked ravioli from the water with a slotted spoon and drain well. Set the ravioli aside in a bowl in a warm spot. Cook the remaining ravioli and remove them from the water with a slotted spoon. Drain well. Distribute the ravioli among 8 warmed, shallow bowls. Spoon the hot sauce evenly over the ravioli and serve immediately.

Each serving provides:

236	Calories	42 g	Carbohydrate
9 g	Protein	179 mg	Sodium
5 g	Fat	12 mg	Cholesterol
2 g	Dietary Fiber		

Red Rice with Peas

VEGAN

Here is a classic, mild-flavored side dish to accompany any Mexican main course. The peas are not essential, but add a beautiful color contrast and a nice fresh flavor and texture.

Yield: 6 side-dish servings

Olive oil	2	teaspoons
Garlic	3	cloves, minced
Pure chile powder	2	teaspoons
Dried thyme	¼	teaspoon
Uncooked long-grain white rice	1½	cups
Mexican Vegetable Stock*	3	cups
Tomato paste	¼	cup
Salt	¼	teaspoon
Cayenne		A pinch
Shelled peas, fresh or frozen	1	cup

In a heavy-bottomed saucepan with a tight-fitting lid, heat the olive oil over medium-low heat. Sauté the garlic with the chile powder and thyme for 1 to 2 minutes, then stir in the rice. Stir and cook 5 minutes.

Meanwhile, thoroughly dissolve the tomato paste in ½ cup of the stock. Add the remaining 2½ cups stock, the salt, and cayenne. Add the stock mixture to the rice and bring to a strong simmer over high heat. Cover the pan, reduce heat to very low, and cook 15 minutes. Pour the peas on top of the rice, and

*If you do not have Mexican Vegetable Stock on hand, make a batch according to the directions on page 38, or dissolve 1 large low-sodium vegetable broth cube in 3 cups of hot water.

The Best 125 Meatless Mexican Dishes

replace the lid. Cook 5 more minutes, until the liquid is absorbed and the rice is tender. Turn off the heat and allow to stand with the lid in place for at least 5 minutes before serving. Serve hot.

Each serving provides:

223	Calories	45 g	Carbohydrate
6 g	Protein	234 mg	Sodium
2 g	Fat	0 mg	Cholesterol
2 g	Dietary Fiber		

Green Rice

VEGAN

This aromatic rice dish is a lovely accompaniment to any robust tomato-based main dish, such as the Potato, Zucchini, and Olive Stew with Garlic, Jalapeños, and Tomatoes (page 153). It is a delicious alternative to the more familiar red Mexican rice.

Yield: 6 side-dish servings

Fresh serrano chile	1	**medium**
Fresh cilantro leaves	1	**cup**
Green onions	6	**medium, minced**
Garlic	3	**cloves, chopped**
Salt	¼	**teaspoon**
Mexican Vegetable Stock*	3	**cups**
Olive oil	2	**teaspoons**
Uncooked long-grain white rice	1½	**cups**
Shelled peas, fresh or frozen	1	**cup**

Remove and discard the stem of the chile, along with the seeds if you prefer a milder dish. In a blender, thoroughly purée the chile, cilantro, green onions, garlic, and salt. Add the stock, 1 cup at a time, blending after each addition.

Heat the olive oil over medium heat in a heavy-bottomed saucepan with a tight-fitting lid and add the rice. Sauté for a few minutes, stirring constantly, to lightly toast the rice. Slowly stir the blended mixture into the saucepan, cover, reduce heat to

*If you do not have Mexican Vegetable Stock on hand, make a batch according to the directions on page 38, or dissolve 1 large low-sodium vegetable broth cube in 3 cups of hot water.

very low, and cook 15 minutes. Distribute the peas on top of the rice, replace the lid, and cook 5 minutes longer. Turn off the heat and allow to stand with the lid in place for at least 5 minutes before serving. Serve hot.

Each serving provides:

221	Calories	45 g	Carbohydrate
6 g	Protein	151 mg	Sodium
2 g	Fat	0 mg	Cholesterol
2 g	Dietary Fiber		

Serrano Chile Rice

VEGAN

We can never decide which side-dish rice is our true favorite, but this one vies for top honors. The chile strips make it as pretty as it is delicious, and, of course, add a bit of heat. Good friend and professional chef Lynn Hager, who has traveled and dined in many parts of Mexico, says this is the best rice she has ever tasted.

Yield: 6 side-dish servings

Fresh serrano chiles	4	**medium**
Olive oil	2	**teaspoons**
Pure chile powder	1	**teaspoon**
Uncooked long-grain white rice	1½	**cups**
Garlic	2	**cloves, minced**
Mexican Vegetable Stock*	2½	**cups**
Tomato juice	½	**cup**
Dried Mexican oregano	1	**teaspoon**
Salt	½	**teaspoon**

Remove and discard the stems of the chiles and scrape out the seeds for a milder dish. Sliver the chiles lengthwise and set the slivers aside.

Heat the oil in a heavy-bottomed saucepan with a tight-fitting lid over medium heat. Add the chile powder and stir around in the pan for about 30 seconds, then add the rice and stir to coat it with the oil and chile powder. Cook, stirring frequently, for about 3 minutes, to toast the rice a bit. Stir in the garlic, then add the stock, tomato juice, oregano, and salt.

---

*If you do not have Mexican Vegetable Stock on hand, make a batch according to the directions on page 38, or dissolve 1 large low-sodium vegetable broth cube in 2½ cups of hot water.

The Best 125 Meatless Mexican Dishes

Stir to combine and bring to a strong simmer over high heat. Cover the pan, reduce heat to very low, and cook 15 minutes. Remove the lid, distribute the chile slivers over the rice, and quickly replace the lid. Cook an additional 5 minutes, then allow to stand with the lid in place for at least 5 minutes before serving. Stir the chile strips into the rice and serve hot.

Each serving provides:

208	Calories	43 g	Carbohydrate
5 g	Protein	278 mg	Sodium
2 g	Fat	0 mg	Cholesterol
1 g	Dietary Fiber		

Mild Rice with Green Beans

VEGAN

This tasty, color-flecked side dish is a favorite of children and others who do not enjoy strong spices. Or think of it as the perfect balance for a spicy main course. In addition to a bright color note, the green beans add an interesting nutty flavor.

Yield: 6 side-dish servings

Fresh green beans	½	**pound**
Canola oil	2	**teaspoons**
White onion	1	**medium, finely diced**
Uncooked long-grain white rice	1½	**cups**
Ground cumin	1½	**teaspoons**
Garlic	1	**clove, minced**
Mexican Vegetable Stock*	3	**cups**
Canned tomatoes, drained and chopped	1	**cup**
Dried Mexican oregano	2	**teaspoons**
Salt	¼	**teaspoon**
Black pepper		**A few grinds**

Rinse the green beans, remove the stems ends, and pull off strings, if necessary. Chop the beans into roughly 1-inch pieces. Set aside.

Heat the oil over medium heat in a heavy-bottomed sauté pan or Dutch oven with a tight-fitting lid. Add the onion and sauté, stirring frequently, until it becomes opaque, about 4 min-

---

*If you do not have Mexican Vegetable Stock on hand, make a batch according to the directions on page 38, or dissolve 1 large low-sodium vegetable broth cube in 3 cups of hot water.

utes. Stir in the rice, then add the cumin and garlic. Cook, stirring frequently, 3 to 4 minutes, to toast the rice and seasonings. Add the stock, green beans, tomatoes, oregano, salt, and pepper. Bring to a strong simmer over high heat, then cover the pan, reduce heat to very low, and cook 20 minutes. Turn off the heat and allow to stand with the lid in place for at least 5 minutes before serving. Serve hot.

Each serving provides:

223	Calories	46 g	Carbohydrate
5 g	Protein	186 mg	Sodium
2 g	Fat	0 mg	Cholesterol
2 g	Dietary Fiber		

Yellow Rice and Pinto Beans

VEGAN

Yellow rice is a popular dish in the Yucatán peninsula of Mexico. Ground annatto seeds are traditionally used to provide the color and a little flavor. The seeds are difficult to find here in the U.S., so this recipe calls for safflower threads. They are the stamen of the safflower plant, similar to saffron threads, but less expensive.

Yield: 6 side-dish servings

Fresh serrano chile	1	**medium**
Uncooked long-grain white rice	1	**cup**
Safflower threads	¼	**teaspoon**
Olive oil	1	**tablespoon**
White onion, chopped	½	**cup**
Cooked pinto beans*	1½	**cups, drained**
Fresh cilantro leaves, minced	2	**tablespoons**

Remove and discard the stem of the chile and scrape out the seeds for a milder dish. Finely mince the chile and set aside.

Bring 2 cups of water to a boil in a medium saucepan that has a tight-fitting lid. Add the rice, chile, and safflower threads. Return to a boil, cover, reduce the heat to low, and cook 20 minutes, until the rice is tender and all the liquid has been absorbed.

---

* Cook beans according to the directions on page 31, or use canned beans that do not contain additives.

Meanwhile, heat the olive oil in a skillet over medium-high heat. Add the onion and sauté for 2 to 3 minutes, until the onion is translucent. Stir in the beans and heat through for about 3 minutes. Add the cooked rice and cilantro and stir to combine. Transfer to a warm bowl and serve immediately.

Each serving provides:

203	Calories	38 g	Carbohydrate
6 g	Protein	3 mg	Sodium
3 g	Fat	0 mg	Cholesterol
2 g	Dietary Fiber		

Baked Rice with Black Beans, Corn, Tomatoes, and Epazote

VEGAN

This delicious dish could serve as a hearty and casual entrée, with the addition of warm corn tortillas and a green salad, or as a side dish with tacos or enchiladas. This recipe makes enough for a crowd—perfect for a party. Leftovers, if there are any, may be stored in a covered container in the refrigerator and enjoyed over the course of a few days, or freeze them for longer periods.

Yield: 12 side-dish servings

Fresh serrano chiles	2	**medium**
Cumin seeds	1	**teaspoon**
Canola oil	1	**tablespoon**
White onion	1	**medium, diced**
Uncooked long-grain white rice	1½	**cups**
Garlic	2	**cloves, minced**
Dried Mexican oregano	2	**teaspoons**
Canned whole tomatoes	1	**28-ounce can**
Mexican Vegetable Stock*	1⅔	**cups**
Corn kernels, fresh or frozen**	2	**cups**
Cooked black beans†	2	**cups, drained**
Fresh epazote leaves, chopped	⅓	**cup**
Salt	¼	**teaspoon**

*If you do not have Mexican Vegetable Stock on hand, make a batch according to the directions on page 38, or dissolve ½ large low-sodium vegetable broth cube in 1⅔ cups of hot water.

**If you are using fresh corn, you will need about 4 medium ears to yield 2 cups of kernels.

†Cook beans according to the directions on page 31, or use canned beans that do not contain additives.

If you have a high-walled Dutch oven that can go directly from the stovetop to the oven, use it for this dish. Otherwise, you may use a stockpot or large saucepan for the first stage, then transfer the mixture to a 3-quart covered casserole dish for baking.

Remove and discard the stems of the chiles and scrape out the seeds for a milder dish. Finely mince the chiles and set aside.

Preheat the oven to 375 degrees F. Crush the cumin seeds thoroughly in a mortar and pestle. Heat the oil in a Dutch oven or stockpot over medium heat. Add the onion and sauté, stirring frequently, 3 to 4 minutes, until the onion is translucent. Stir in the rice, then add the garlic, oregano, and cumin seeds and stir and sauté 3 to 4 minutes. Add the undrained tomatoes and the stock, then stir in the corn, beans, chiles, epazote, and salt.

Bring to a strong simmer over high heat, then cover the pan (or transfer the mixture to the covered casserole dish) and bake for 30 minutes. Remove from the oven and allow to stand at room temperature for 10 minutes before serving. Serve hot, drizzled with Mexican Crema (page 33), if desired.

━━ ━━ ━━ ━━ ━━ ━━ ━━ ━━ ━━ ━━

Each serving provides:

189	Calories	38 g	Carbohydrate
6 g	Protein	171 mg	Sodium
2 g	Fat	0 mg	Cholesterol
3 g	Dietary Fiber		

Pasta with Poblano and Cinnamon Sauce

ALMOST INSTANT

This pasta dish has a homey, comfort-food quality—a velvety smooth texture and a spicy flavor with just a hint of sweetness. Once the chiles are roasted, it comes together very quickly. We find that the small elbow pasta, called condito *in Mexican markets, works best in this dish.*

Yield: 6 side-dish servings

Fresh poblano chiles	2	**large (½ pound)**
Olive oil	2	**tablespoons**
Garlic	1	**clove**
Dried marjoram	½	**teaspoon**
Ground cinnamon	¼	**teaspoon**
Lowfat Crema (page 34)	½	**cup**
Small elbow pasta	7	**ounces**

Roast the chiles over a gas burner, under a broiler, or on a hot grill, turning frequently until the skin is charred black and the chiles have begun to collapse. Place them immediately into a paper or plastic bag and fold the bag closed; set aside.

Bring several quarts of water to a boil for the pasta. When the roasted chiles are cool enough to handle, discard the skins, stems, and seeds, and place the pulp in a food processor. Add the olive oil, garlic, marjoram, and cinnamon. Purée until smooth. Add the crema and blend again, then set aside in a warm spot.

Cook the pasta in the boiling water until al dente. Drain the pasta and place it in a large warmed serving bowl. Top with the sauce, toss, and serve immediately. The heat of the pasta will warm up the sauce.

Each serving provides:

193	Calories	27 g	Carbohydrate
5 g	Protein	12 mg	Sodium
8 g	Fat	8 mg	Cholesterol
3 g	Dietary Fiber		

Pasta with Grilled Tomato Sauce

VEGAN

The grilled vegetables make this tomato sauce a special flavor treat. It makes a simple, delicious, and elegant side dish for a dinner party.

Yield: 8 side-dish servings

Fresh pear tomatoes	**2½**	**pounds**
Yellow onions	**2**	**medium**
Garlic	**1**	**large bulb**
Olive oil	**1**	**tablespoon**
Dried Mexican oregano	**1**	**tablespoon**
Dried fideos (coiled vermicelli)	**14**	**ounces**

Preheat a coal or gas grill to medium. Remove and discard the stem ends of the tomatoes, but leave them whole. Peel the onions and cut them in half. Break the bulb of garlic into individual cloves and peel them. Lightly oil the onions and garlic cloves with the olive oil. Place the onions on the grill, cut side down, along with the tomatoes. Grill for about 30 minutes, turning occasionally, until tender. The onions and tomatoes will char slightly. Put the garlic on the grill during the last 10 minutes of cooking time, either in a grill basket or on a fine grill rack. Place the cooked vegetables and garlic in a food processor and purée. Add the oregano and pulse again.

Meanwhile, bring several quarts of water to a boil in a large stockpot and cook the pasta until al dente. Drain the pasta well and place it in a warm, large serving bowl. Top with the sauce, toss gently, and serve immediately.

Each serving provides:

257	Calories	50 g	Carbohydrate
8 g	Protein	13 mg	Sodium
3 g	Fat	0 mg	Cholesterol
5 g	Dietary Fiber		

Pasta with Cilantro Pesto and Avocado

Cilantro fans will become addicted to this pesto. The roasted garlic imparts a mellow, sweet flavor.

Yield: 6 main-dish servings

Garlic	1	large bulb
Raw unsalted pumpkin seeds	¼	cup plus 2 tablespoons
Fresh cilantro leaves	1½	cups
Fresh parsley leaves	1½	cups
Olive oil	⅓	cup
Pure chile powder	2	teaspoons
Dried red chile flakes	1	teaspoon
Ground cumin	1	teaspoon
Fresh-squeezed lemon juice	¼	cup
Lowfat Crema (page 34)	½	cup
Dried spiral pasta	12	ounces
Ripe Haas avocado	1	medium (½ pound)
Red bell pepper	1	medium, diced

Preheat the oven to 350 degrees F. Trim ¼-inch off the top end of the garlic bulb to just expose the individual cloves. Wrap with foil or place in a ceramic garlic baker and bake for 45 minutes. The garlic inside the skin will soften to a paste-like consistency. Allow it to cool for a few minutes before squeezing the garlic paste from the cloves.

Meanwhile, toast the pumpkin seeds by placing them in a dry heavy-bottomed skillet over medium heat. Shake the pan frequently so the seeds toast evenly, but do not burn. They will begin to pop and turn golden brown. Remove them from the pan and set aside.

Bring several quarts of water to a boil for the pasta. Meanwhile, wash the cilantro and parsley and dry well. In a food processor or blender, combine the cilantro, parsley, and olive oil. Purée to the consistency of a thick paste. Add the garlic paste, chile powder, chile flakes, cumin, a heaping ¼ cup of the pumpkin seeds (they expand when they are toasted), and the lemon juice. (Reserve the remaining seeds to garnish the pasta.) Purée until fairly smooth and set aside.

Cook the pasta in the boiling water until al dente. Meanwhile, in a small saucepan, stir together the cilantro mixture and the crema to make the pesto. Warm over very low heat until hot but not simmering.

Cut the avocado open and remove the pit (see page 6). Peel the avocado and slice it.

Drain the pasta well and place it in a warmed serving bowl. Toss with the pesto and diced bell pepper. Serve immediately, garnished with the avocado slices and remaining pumpkin seeds.

Each serving provides:

514	Calories	62 g	Carbohydrate
14 g	Protein	94 mg	Sodium
25 g	Fat	8 mg	Cholesterol
7 g	Dietary Fiber		

Pasta with Browned Onions, Cauliflower, Serrano Chile, and Mint

ALMOST INSTANT

This quick-to-fix vegetable-laden pasta dish is nutritious, hearty, spicy, and scrumptious. You may use Mexican añejo or Romano cheese in place of the dry Jack. An excellent side dish for this pasta is Zucchini and Mushrooms in Spicy Lime Marinade (page 112).

Yield: 4 main-dish servings

Fresh serrano chile	1	**medium**
White onion	1	**medium**
Red onion	1	**medium**
Canola oil	1	**tablespoon**
Fresh cauliflower, diced	3	**cups (about ¾ pound)**
Garlic	2	**cloves, minced**
Pure chile powder	2	**teaspoons**
Ground cumin	1	**teaspoon**
Salt		**A pinch**
Dried fettuccine	8	**ounces**
Dry Jack cheese, finely grated	¼	**cup**
Lowfat Crema (page 34)	½	**cup**
Fresh mint leaves, slivered	½	**cup**

Remove and discard the stem of the chile and scrape out the seeds for a milder dish. Finely mince the chile and set aside. Bring several quarts of water to a boil for the pasta.

Meanwhile, peel the onions, trim off and discard the ends, and cut the onions in half from root to stem end. Cut each half crosswise into ¼-inch slices. Heat the oil over medium heat in a heavy-bottomed skillet or Dutch oven that has a tight-fitting lid. Sauté the onions for 10 minutes, stirring frequently. Stir in the cauliflower, chile, garlic, chile powder, cumin, and salt. Add 1 cup of water and immediately cover the pan. Cook 7 to 10 minutes, until the cauliflower is fork-tender.

Meanwhile, cook the fettuccine in the boiling water until al dente. Stir the cheese and crema together in a large, warmed serving bowl, then slowly stir in 2 tablespoons of the pasta cooking water to warm the mixture just a bit. Drain the pasta briefly and add it to the sauce in the bowl. Toss briefly, then add the cauliflower mixture and mint and toss again until well combined. Serve very hot.

Each serving provides:

385	Calories	61 g	Carbohydrate
14 g	Protein	108 mg	Sodium
10 g	Fat	17 mg	Cholesterol
7 g	Dietary Fiber		

Pasta and Broccoli with Creamy Spiced Tomato Sauce

ALMOST INSTANT

Prepare this quick and delicious standby whenever you are in a rush to get a meal on the table. Put the pasta water on to boil and 20 minutes later you'll be serving a wonderful, nutritious meal.

Yield: 6 main-dish servings

Fresh pear tomatoes	¾	**pound**
Lowfat Crema (page 34)	¾	**cup**
Plain nonfat yogurt	¾	**cup**
Chopped black olives	1	**4¼-ounce can**
Fresh cilantro leaves, minced	¼	**cup**
Pure chile powder	1	**tablespoon**
Dried Mexican oregano	2	**teaspoons**
Garlic	3	**cloves, minced**
Salt	¼	**teaspoon**
Black pepper		**Several grinds**
Fresh broccoli	1	**pound**
Dried pasta spirals	12	**ounces**
Romano cheese, finely grated	¼	**cup**

Put several quarts of water on to boil for the pasta. Meanwhile, cut out the stem ends of the tomatoes and cut them in half crosswise. Squeeze the tomatoes over the sink to remove the juicy seed pockets, then finely dice them. In a medium saucepan, combine the tomatoes, crema, yogurt, olives, cilantro, chile powder, oregano, garlic, salt, and pepper. Cook over medium heat for 15 minutes, stirring frequently.

Meanwhile, trim off and discard the tough stem ends of the broccoli. Peel the remaining stalks if they are particularly thick-skinned. Chop the stalks and heads into small, uniform pieces. Cook the pasta in the boiling water until al dente, adding the broccoli for the last 4 minutes. Drain well and toss with the hot sauce and Romano cheese. Serve immediately in warmed bowls.

Each serving provides:

324	Calories	51 g	Carbohydrate
13 g	Protein	376 mg	Sodium
8 g	Fat	16 mg	Cholesterol
7 g	Dietary Fiber		

Pasta and Acorn Squash with Chipotle Chile Cheese Sauce

This thoroughly satisfying Mexican mac-and-cheese is a surefire hit. To make a milder version, suitable for children, use only 1 chipotle chile and 1 tablespoon of adobo sauce. You may, of course, use a commercially prepared salsa fresca if you do not wish to take the time to make it from scratch.

Yield: 6 main-dish servings

Salsa Fresca (page 56)	¾	**cup**
Lowfat milk	2½	**cups**
Acorn squash	1	**medium (1½ pounds)**
Dried penne or rigatoni	12	**ounces**
Canola oil	1	**tablespoon**
White onion	1	**medium, diced**
Chipotle chiles en adobo	2	**medium**
Unbleached flour	2	**tablespoons**
Adobo sauce from canned chipotles	2	**tablespoons**
Fresh cilantro leaves, minced	⅓	**cup**
Sharp cheddar cheese, shredded	8	**ounces (2 cups)**
Salt		**A pinch**

Put several quarts of water on to boil. If you're using salsa fresca that has been refrigerated, set it out at room temperature while you prepare the dish. Place the milk in a saucepan over low heat and heat until steaming, but do not bring to a boil.

Meanwhile, cut the squash in half and scrape out the seeds. Slice the squash halves into wedges and peel them. Dice the squash and set aside. When the water for the pasta is boiling rapidly, stir in the pasta and return to a boil. Cook 5 minutes, stirring occasionally, then add the diced squash to the pot. Return to a boil and cook until the pasta is al dente and the squash is fork-tender, 6 to 8 minutes. Drain very well.

While the pasta is cooking, heat the oil over medium heat in a heavy-bottomed saucepan. Add the onion and sauté 3 to 4 minutes, until it begins to soften. Add the chiles, coated with sauce, and use a wooden spoon to thoroughly mash them against the bottom of the pan into very small bits. Reduce the heat to medium-low and add the flour. Cook, stirring constantly, about 2 minutes to brown the flour a little. Add about ¾ cup of the warmed milk and stir well. Bring to a simmer over medium heat. When thickened, add the remaining milk, adobo sauce, and cilantro. Simmer over medium heat, stirring frequently, until the sauce is the consistency of thick cream.

When the pasta and squash are cooked, drain them and transfer to a warmed serving bowl. Add the sauce and cheese and toss to combine. Serve hot, topping each serving with 2 tablespoons of the salsa fresca.

Each serving provides:

473	Calories	58 g	Carbohydrate
21 g	Protein	436 mg	Sodium
18 g	Fat	43 mg	Cholesterol
7 g	Dietary Fiber		

Bean Dishes

Beans, or *frijoles,* are among the most ancient foods of Mexico, and still appear on most family tables daily. Various dried beans are enjoyed in different regions, but the pinto bean and black bean are probably the most popular.

A steaming pot of simmering beans is a common sight in Mexican kitchens. We have provided a recipe in this chapter for these everyday pot beans. Though each Mexican cook has his or her own treasured recipe, ours is representative: The beans are not strongly seasoned and not overcooked, which enhances their versatility.

Beans cooked at home have a better flavor and texture than commercially canned beans, and they're more economical. We provide detailed instructions for cooking dried beans on page 31. We frequently cook more than we need and freeze the surplus in measured amounts. This is a convenient way to keep cooked beans on hand for those times when sudden inspiration strikes. If you do use canned beans, look for a brand that does not contain additives.

Beans are nourishing, hearty fare that deserve an important role in all North American diets. These Mexican-inspired side dishes are delicious enough to become part of your repertoire of favorite recipes.

Tips and Tools

- For cooking beans in large quantities, you will need a large stockpot and long-handled wooden spoon.
- A cast-iron skillet or other heavy-bottomed skillet is preferred for frying beans. It should not have a nonstick surface, since you will be scraping the bottom of the pan as the beans cook down.
- Marinated beans are a wonderful make-ahead appetizer or side dish. A day or two in the refrigerator may even improve the flavor, but return the mixture to room temperature before serving.
- Fresh-cooked beans can be held in their cooking liquid in the refrigerator for up to 3 days before using them in a recipe, or freeze them in measured amounts for longer periods.

Basic Pot Beans

VEGAN

This is a version of everyday pot beans, or frijoles de olla, *as enjoyed throughout Mexico. The beans are barely seasoned while cooking, so they lend themselves to many uses. They might be enjoyed right out of the pot—put into heavy clay bowls and topped with a favorite salsa. Frequently they are made into* refritos *(which translates to "well-fried," not "refried" as is commonly assumed). Pinto beans are a national favorite, but pink, kidney, or black beans also work well. Cooking time varies for dried beans, depending on the variety and the age of the bean, hence the broad range given in this recipe.*

Yield: 6½ cups

Dried pinto beans	1	**pound (about 2½ cups)**
Garlic	1	**large clove**
Salt	1	**teaspoon**

Sort through the pinto beans, discarding any pebbles or other foreign objects. Briefly rinse the beans and place them in a heavy stockpot. Add 8 cups of water, cover the pot, and allow to soak for several hours or overnight. (Alternatively, you may bring the water to a boil, then add the beans, turn off the heat, cover the pot, and soak only 2 hours.)

Peel and crush the garlic clove and set it aside. Drain the soaked beans and return them to the stockpot. Add water to submerge them by a depth of about 1 inch (6 cups should do it). Bring the beans to a rolling boil over high heat. Add the crushed garlic clove and reduce the heat to medium-low to maintain a moderate simmer. Cover the pot and cook 30 minutes.

Remove the lid, stir, and add 1 cup of very hot water. Replace the lid, return to a simmer, and cook 45 minutes. Add a little additional hot water, if needed, to keep the beans barely covered, and add the salt. Cook, covered, an additional 15 to 45 minutes, until the beans are very tender but not mushy. Serve as is, or use in your favorite bean dish. Freeze any beans that will not be used within a couple days.

Each ½-cup serving provides:

62	Calories	12 g	Carbohydrate
4 g	Protein	166 mg	Sodium
0 g	Fat	0 mg	Cholesterol
2 g	Dietary Fiber		

Simple Refritos with Onion and Oregano

ALMOST INSTANT, VEGAN

Every Mexican family has its own favorite version of "well-fried" beans. Here is one that is delicious and simple—a classic Mexican side dish. The beans can be served hot or at room temperature, as a dip for chips, and perhaps sprinkled with Parmesan cheese and minced pickled jalapeños. If serving the beans as a hot side dish, you may stir in some crumbled queso fresco, if you wish. Cooled beans can be frozen for future use.

Yield: 6 side-dish servings

Cooked pinto beans*	4	**cups, drained**
Bean cooking or canning liquid	1	**cup**
Canola oil	3	**tablespoons**
White onion, minced	1	**cup**
Dried Mexican oregano	1	**tablespoon**
Salt	½	**teaspoon**
Black pepper		**Several grinds**

In a blender or food processor, purée the beans with the bean liquid until fairly smooth. Heat the oil in a heavy-bottomed skillet over medium heat and sauté the onion, stirring frequently, until it begins to brown. Add the puréed beans,

*Cook dried beans according to the directions on page 284, or use canned beans that do not contain additives.

oregano, salt, and pepper. Reduce heat to medium-low and cook, stirring and scraping the pan frequently, until the beans thicken up and pull away from the sides of the pan when stirred, about 10 minutes. Serve hot or at room temperature, garnished as desired.

Each serving provides:

388	Calories	61 g	Carbohydrate
19 g	Protein	182 mg	Sodium
8 g	Fat	0 mg	Cholesterol
10 g	Dietary Fiber		

Refritos with Garlic, Chipotle Chile, and Beer

ALMOST INSTANT

This pungent concoction is a delicious side dish, but can also become a filling for burritos or a tostada topping. Pour the beer into a glass and allow it to stand at room temperature for several hours before using. The 1 tablespoon minced chipotle chile will lend a smoky goodness to the dish; 2 tablespoons will fire it up nicely.

Yield: 6 side-dish servings

Unsalted butter	2	**tablespoons**
Fresh cilantro leaves, minced	¼	**cup**
Garlic	3	**cloves, minced**
Chipotle chile en adobo, minced	1	**tablespoon**
Cooked pinto beans*	4	**cups, drained**
Bean cooking or canning liquid	½	**cup**
Flat beer	½	**cup**
Salt	½	**teaspoon**

Melt the butter in a heavy-bottomed skillet over medium heat. Add the cilantro, garlic, and chile and stir briefly. Then add the beans, bean cooking liquid, beer, and salt. Bring to a strong simmer, then reduce the heat to medium-low to maintain a moderate simmer. Cook for about 10 minutes, mashing the beans with a potato masher as they heat up. Only mash about

*Cook dried beans according to the directions on page 284, or use canned beans that do not contain additives.

half the beans; you don't want a perfectly smooth texture. Cook until the beans are an appetizing texture—soupy or dry, as you wish. If you are serving the beans as a side dish, you will want a more liquid texture. For burritos or tostadas, a somewhat drier texture is preferred.

Each serving provides:

355	Calories	59 g	Carbohydrate
19 g	Protein	207 mg	Sodium
5 g	Fat	11 mg	Cholesterol
9 g	Dietary Fiber		

Refried Black Beans

ALMOST INSTANT, VEGAN

*In traditional Mexican recipes, the fat used for refried beans is pork
lard, which contributes its flavor to the beans. With black beans, we
use an extra virgin olive oil instead. The oil, like lard, keeps the beans
from drying out. The freshly ground cumin seeds add a flavor that
is more pronounced than the preground version.*

Yield: 6 side-dish servings

Cumin seeds	½	**teaspoon**
Extra virgin olive oil	1	**tablespoon**
Yellow onion, minced	½	**cup**
Pure chile powder	¼	**teaspoon**
Cooked black beans*	2½	**cups**
Bean cooking or canning liquid	2	**tablespoons**

Crush the cumin seeds thoroughly with a mortar and pestle
and set aside. Heat the olive oil in a heavy-bottomed skillet
over medium heat. Add the onion and sauté for 2 to 3 minutes,
until it begins to soften. Add the cumin and chile powder. Continue to cook for about a minute, then increase the heat to
medium-high and stir in about a third of the beans, along with
the bean cooking liquid. Mash them with a potato masher or the

*Cook dried beans according to the directions on page 31, or use canned beans
that do not contain additives.

back of a wooden spoon. Add another third of the beans and mash them in the same manner. Stir in the remaining third of the beans and mash again. Continue to cook for about 5 minutes, stirring almost constantly, until the beans are very hot. Serve immediately.

Each serving provides:

120	Calories	18 g	Carbohydrate
7 g	Protein	2 mg	Sodium
3 g	Fat	0 mg	Cholesterol
3 g	Dietary Fiber		

Whole Pinto Beans
with Minced Vegetables

VEGAN

This dish has become one of our favorite accompaniments to Mexican entrées. The beans also make a delicious casual lunch, eaten steaming hot from a deep bowl with warmed corn tortillas on the side.

Yield: 6 side-dish servings

Fresh serrano chiles	2	medium
Red or yellow bell pepper	1	medium, minced
White onion	1	medium, minced
Carrot	1	medium, minced
Zucchini	1	medium, minced
Canola oil	1	tablespoon
Garlic	2	cloves, minced
Dried Mexican oregano	2	tablespoons
Cooked pinto beans*	4	cups, drained
Canned whole tomatoes, chopped and drained	1	cup
Bean cooking or canning liquid	¼	cup
Fresh cilantro leaves, minced	½	cup

*Cook dried beans according to the directions on page 284, or use canned beans that do not contain additives.

Remove and discard the stem of the chiles, and scrape out the seeds for a milder dish. Finely mince the chiles and set them aside.

Heat the oil in a deep heavy-bottomed skillet over medium heat. Add all the vegetables, the chiles, the garlic, and 1 tablespoon of the oregano and sauté for 10 minutes, stirring frequently. (It is fine if the vegetables brown a bit.) Add the beans, tomatoes, and bean cooking liquid and cook, stirring frequently, 10 minutes. Stir in the cilantro and the remaining 1 tablespoon oregano and serve hot.

Each serving provides:

378	Calories	68 g	Carbohydrate
21 g	Protein	80 mg	Sodium
4 g	Fat	0 mg	Cholesterol
11 g	Dietary Fiber		

Marinated Garbanzo Beans with Roasted Garlic, Tomatoes, and Capers

VEGAN

Garbanzo beans, also called chickpeas, are enjoyed in some parts of Mexico. This recipe for garbanzo beans makes plenty of marinade; serve the beans in shallow bowls, along with thick country bread, a bowl of olives, and a favorite cheese. This would make a wonderful lunch, or—in smaller portions, of course—a memorable first course or side dish at dinner time.

Yield: 8 side-dish servings

Fresh serrano chile	1	**medium**
Olive oil	1	**tablespoon plus 1 teaspoon**
Fresh tomatoes	2	**large (about 1 pound)**
Garlic	6	**large cloves**
Fresh-squeezed lime juice	2	**tablespoons**
Dried Mexican oregano	1	**teaspoon**
Salt	¼	**teaspoon**
Capers, drained and chopped if large	3	**tablespoons**
Cooked garbanzo beans*	2½	**cups, drained**
Red onion	½	**medium, thinly sliced**

*Cook dried beans according to the directions on page 31, or use canned beans that do not contain additives.

Remove and discard the stem of the chile and scrape out the seeds for a milder dish. Finely mince the chile and set it aside.

Preheat the broiler. Rub a small, heavy, ovenproof skillet with the 1 teaspoon oil and set the tomatoes in the skillet. Place the skillet about 6 inches away from the broiler and cook the tomatoes 10 to 12 minutes, turning them once in the middle of the cooking time. The tomatoes should be charred and softened somewhat. Transfer them to a bowl and set aside.

Meanwhile, heat a cast-iron griddle or heavy-bottomed skillet over medium-high heat. Pierce each garlic clove once with a fork and place the whole unpeeled cloves on the hot griddle. Roast, turning frequently, until the cloves are very soft, 10 to 15 minutes. Remove them from the pan and set aside. When the garlic is cool enough to handle, squeeze it out of its skin into a small bowl.

Add the 1 tablespoon olive oil, the lime juice, oregano, and salt to the garlic and whisk until well combined. With a wooden spoon, gently press on the tomatoes in the bowl to release most of their juice. Pour the juice into the garlic mixture and whisk together. Stir in the capers and chile and set it aside.

Peel off and discard the skin of the tomatoes. Chop the tomatoes coarsely. Toss the garbanzos with the tomatoes and the red onion, then with the garlic mixture. Serve immediately or allow to stand at room temperature for up to several hours before serving, stirring occasionally.

━ ━━ ━ ━━ ━ ━━ ━ ━━ ━

Each serving provides:

133	Calories	20 g	Carbohydrate
6 g	Protein	152 mg	Sodium
4 g	Fat	0 mg	Cholesterol
3 g	Dietary Fiber		

White Beans with Tomatoes and Serrano Chiles

VEGAN

These white beans have a moist texture and unique slightly spicy, smoky flavor. Combine them on a menu with Green Rice (page 260) and Chard and Poblano Chile Enchiladas with Tomatillo Sauce (page 197) for a memorable feast.

Yield: 8 side-dish servings

Dried small white beans	1	**cup**
Fresh tomatoes	2	**medium (about 1 pound)**
Canola oil	1	**tablespoon**
White onion	1	**medium, chopped**
Garlic	4	**cloves, minced**
Chipotle chiles en adobo, minced	1	**tablespoon**
Salt	½	**teaspoon**

Rinse and sort the beans and place them in a saucepan. Cover with hot water and soak for about 2 hours. Drain off the soaking water and add fresh water to cover. Bring to a boil over high heat, reduce the heat to medium to maintain a moderate simmer, and cook 45 minutes to 1 hour, until the beans are tender.

Meanwhile, blanch the tomatoes by immersing them in rapidly boiling water for 2 to 3 minutes. While the tomatoes are heating, fill a large bowl or basin with ice water. Drain the tomatoes in a colander and immediately plunge them into the ice water. When they are cool enough to handle, peel the tomatoes. Remove and discard the stem ends and cut the tomatoes in half crosswise. Gently squeeze over the sink to remove the juicy seed pockets, then dice the tomatoes and place them in a bowl.

Heat the oil over medium heat in a heavy-bottomed skillet and add the onion and garlic. Sauté for 2 to 3 minutes, until the onion begins to soften. Stir in the tomatoes, chile, and salt. Increase the heat to medium-high and continue to cook for about 5 minutes, stirring occasionally, until the sauce has reduced somewhat. If you are still waiting for the beans to cook, turn off the heat, cover the pan, and set aside.

When the beans are tender, drain them and add them to the sauce. Cook over medium-high heat for 3 to 4 minutes, stirring to combine well. Serve hot.

Each serving provides:

125	Calories	20 g	Carbohydrate
7 g	Protein	165 mg	Sodium
2 g	Fat	0 mg	Cholesterol
2 g	Dietary Fiber		

Lima Beans and Mushrooms in Serrano Chile Tomato Sauce

VEGAN

This recipe uses fresh shiitake mushrooms in an unconventional way. Select fairly large ones, of similar size if possible. If you have cooked beans on hand, this dish comes together quickly and easily and is a great choice for an impromptu dinner party on a chilly evening. Add your favorite side-dish rice and a leafy salad for a wonderful winter feast.

Yield: 4 main-dish servings

Fresh serrano chiles	2	**medium**
Canned whole pear tomatoes	1	**28-ounce can**
Garlic	3	**cloves**
Fresh cilantro leaves	½	**cup**
Fresh-squeezed lime juice	2	**tablespoons**
Salt	¼	**teaspoon plus ⅛ teaspoon**
Fresh shiitake mushrooms	¼	**pound**
Button mushrooms	½	**pound**
Olive oil	2	**tablespoons**
Cooked lima beans*	2	**cups**
Shelled peas, fresh or frozen	1	**cup**
Madeira or dry sherry	¼	**cup**
Black pepper		**Several grinds**

*Cook dried beans according to the directions on page 31, or use thawed frozen lima beans.

Remove and discard the stems of the chiles and scrape out the seeds for a milder dish. Finely mince the chiles and set them aside. In a blender, combine the chiles, undrained tomatoes, garlic, cilantro, lime juice, and the ⅛ teaspoon salt. Purée to a smooth consistency and set aside. Gently wipe the mushrooms clean with a damp tea towel. Cut the shiitakes into ¼-inch slices. Quarter the button mushrooms.

Heat the oil over medium heat in a heavy-bottomed skillet or Dutch oven. Add the mushrooms and sauté for 3 to 4 minutes, until they begin to turn golden. Add the tomato mixture—careful, it will splatter—and the lima beans. Cook over medium-low heat, stirring frequently, about 15 minutes, until the sauce has reduced to a nice, thick consistency. If you are using fresh shelled peas, add them for the last 5 to 6 minutes of cooking time. If you are using frozen peas, rinse briefly to melt the ice crystals, drain, and add them for the last 2 minutes of cooking time. Stir in the Madeira and pepper and heat through for another minute. Serve very hot.

━ ━━ ━ ━━ ━ ━ ━ ━━ ━

Each serving provides:

296	Calories	44 g	Carbohydrate
14 g	Protein	598 mg	Sodium
8 g	Fat	0 mg	Cholesterol
10 g	Dietary Fiber		

Hot Vegetable Side Dishes

Since pre-Columbian times, vegetables have been at the center of Meso-American cuisine. Tomatoes, beans, squash, mushrooms, corn—these age-old vegetables still play a dominant role in Mexican cooking.

Many traditional Mexican main-course dishes are laden with vegetables. Vegetables also are enjoyed in condiments, sauces, and soups. In this chapter, we present an array of vegetable side dishes that can accompany any number of entrées.

Most of the vegetables used here are readily available, in season, throughout the U.S. The less common ingredients—chayotes, tomatillos, and plantains—may be available only in specialty markets, but are worth seeking out. The index will guide you to pages that discuss these unfamiliar foods.

Many of these delicious dishes are quick to fix and can be prepared while waiting for the casserole to bake or the sauce to simmer. And they have another added bonus: They help us fulfill the nutritionist's recommendation to eat lots of vegetables.

Tips and Tools

- Most vegetables taste best when cooked only until fork-tender, retaining some firmness but easy to pierce with a fork. Overcooking renders many vegetables unappetizing in flavor and texture, so test frequently and remove them from the heat as soon as they are tender.

- A collapsible steaming tray made of perforated stainless steel and a pot with a tight-fitting lid are essential for steaming vegetables.

- A heavy-bottomed sauté pan or cast-iron skillet with a tight-fitting lid are necessary for braising vegetables.

Corn on the Cob with Spicy Cheese Spread

ALMOST INSTANT

In all of Latin America, corn is a staple. It most often finds its way into the diet in the form of tortillas or other masa preparations, which are made from dried corn, but it is also enjoyed fresh when in season. This is a perfect summer barbecue side dish, particularly if the rest of the menu is low in fat.

Yield: 6 side-dish servings

Unsalted butter	3	tablespoons
Parmesan cheese, finely grated	2	tablespoons
Pure chile powder	1	tablespoon
Fresh-squeezed lime juice	2	teaspoons
Granulated garlic	½	teaspoon
Salt	⅛	teaspoon
Fresh corn	6	medium ears

For ease of preparation, leave the butter out to soften at room temperature for an hour or so before making the spread.

Bring 3 quarts of water to a boil in a stockpot over high heat. Meanwhile, add the cheese, chile powder, lime juice, granulated garlic, and salt to the butter in a small bowl and mash with a fork until well incorporated. Transfer to a small serving crock or bowl and set aside at room temperature (or prepare well ahead of time and store, tightly covered, in the refrigerator, but return the spread to room temperature before serving).

Remove and discard the corn husks and silk. Place the corn in the boiling water and cook 5 minutes. Drain well and serve piping hot. Place the spread in the center of the table and give each diner a small spreading knife.

Each serving provides:

150	Calories	20 g	Carbohydrate
4 g	Protein	101 mg	Sodium
8 g	Fat	18 mg	Cholesterol
3 g	Dietary Fiber		

Grilled Artichokes with Chipotle Chile Mayonnaise

Artichokes cooked on the grill have a delightful smoky flavor. We enjoy them served plain or with regular mayonnaise, but the chipotle chile mayonnaise complements the grilled flavor particularly well.

Yield: 4 side-dish servings

Artichokes	**2**	**large**
Olive oil	**2**	**teaspoons**
Chipotle Chile Mayonnaise (page 35)	**½**	**cup**

Trim off and discard about 1 inch of the pointy leaf tips and ¼-inch of the stem from each artichoke. If there are small, tough leaves around the base, remove and discard them. Vigorously swirl artichokes in a basin of water or rinse thoroughly to flush out any earwigs that may be present.

Put a steaming rack in a stockpot and add a few inches of water. Bring the water to a boil over high heat, place the artichokes on the rack, leaves pointing down, and cover the pot. Reduce the heat to medium and steam 25 to 45 minutes, depending on the size of the artichokes. Remove them from the pan when the stems are barely fork-tender, as they will continue to cook on the grill.

Meanwhile, preheat a coal or gas grill to medium-high. When the artichokes are just cool enough to handle, cut them in half lengthwise. Scrape out the fuzzy choke and lightly brush the cut sides with the olive oil, using ¼ teaspoon per artichoke half. Place the artichokes cut side down on the grill and cook for 10 minutes. Arrange on a large platter or on individual serving plates and pass the chipotle chile mayonnaise.

Each serving provides:

222	Calories	8 g	Carbohydrate
3 g	Protein	126 mg	Sodium
21 g	Fat	17 mg	Cholesterol
4 g	Dietary Fiber		

Braised Carrots with Lime Juice and Shallots

ALMOST INSTANT, VEGAN

This simple carrot dish is absolutely scrumptious. Select shallots that are firm and without mold, and store them in a plastic bag in the refrigerator until you use them; they spoil faster than other members of the onion family.

Yield: 4 side-dish servings

Carrots	1	**pound**
Shallots	4	**medium**
Salt	⅛	**teaspoon**
Black pepper		**Several grinds**
Fresh-squeezed lime juice	2	**tablespoons**
Fresh cilantro leaves, minced	2	**tablespoons**

Scrub the carrots; there is no need to peel them. Slice the carrots crosswise at a slant into ½-inch pieces. Set aside. Peel the shallots and slice off the root end. Cut each shallot in half lengthwise and slice each half lengthwise into very thin slivers. Set aside separately.

Place the carrots, salt, and pepper in a heavy-bottomed pan along with ½ cup water, and bring to a simmer over medium-high heat. Cover the pan tightly, reduce the heat to medium-low, and cook 8 minutes. Remove the lid and stir in the shallots and lime juice. Cover and cook an additional 4 minutes. Remove the lid and cook, stirring almost constantly, until all the water is absorbed and the carrots are fork-tender. It is fine for the shallots and carrots to brown a bit, but don't let them scorch.

Transfer the carrots to a serving bowl, scraping the pan lightly with a rubber spatula to remove all the juices and bits of browned shallot. Toss with the cilantro and serve hot or at room temperature.

Each serving provides:

63	Calories	15 g	Carbohydrate
2 g	Protein	139 mg	Sodium
0 g	Fat	0 mg	Cholesterol
2 g	Dietary Fiber		

Cauliflower Braised with Tomatillos, Rosemary, and Red Chile Strips

ALMOST INSTANT

Cauliflower is a most versatile vegetable, as this recipe demonstrates. This dish delivers a powerhouse of flavor and is a great accompaniment to any Mexican entrée.

Yield: 6 side-dish servings

Dried ancho chiles	2	**medium**
Fresh tomatillos	½	**pound (6 medium)**
Unsalted butter	1	**tablespoon**
Garlic	3	**cloves, minced**
Dried rosemary	1	**teaspoon, crushed**
Fresh cauliflower, diced	4	**cups (1 pound)**
Salt	¼	**teaspoon**
Fresh lime wedges	6	

Tear the chiles open and discard the seeds and stems. Use scissors or a knife to cut the chiles into very thin 1-inch strips. Set the strips aside. Peel off and discard the papery husks of the tomatillos. Wash the tomatillos and quarter them. Set aside.

Melt the butter in a heavy-bottomed sauté pan that has a tight-fitting lid. Add the garlic and rosemary and sauté, stirring constantly, 1 minute. Add the tomatillos and cauliflower and stir and sauté 1 minute longer, then add ½ cup of water, the salt, and the chile strips. Immediately cover the pan, reduce the heat to medium-low, and cook 7 to 10 minutes, until the cauliflower is fork-tender. Serve hot or at room temperature, offering lime wedges for squeezing onto the cauliflower.

Each serving provides:

63	Calories	10 g	Carbohydrate
3 g	Protein	105 mg	Sodium
3 g	Fat	6 mg	Cholesterol
3 g	Dietary Fiber		

Green Beans Braised with Chiles and Pumpkin Seeds

Pumpkin seeds are a favorite ingredient in Mexican cooking, treasured for their texture as well as their unique flavor. Here they add a nice crunch.

Yield: 6 side-dish servings

Fresh poblano chiles	2	**medium (½ pound)**
Raw unsalted pumpkin seeds	2	**tablespoons**
Fresh green beans	1	**pound**
Canola oil	1	**tablespoon**
Yellow onion	1	**small, chopped**
Lowfat Crema (page 34)	3	**tablespoons**
Fresh cilantro, minced	2	**tablespoons**

Roast the chiles on a hot grill or under the broiler for about 5 minutes, or until the skin is uniformly charred. Turn and blacken the other side. Place immediately in a plastic or paper bag and fold the bag closed; set aside. The steam inside the bag will finish cooking the chiles. When they are cool enough to handle, remove and discard the skin, stem, and seeds.

Meanwhile, place the pumpkin seeds in a dry heavy-bottomed skillet in a single layer over medium heat. Toast the seeds until they pop and begin to brown. Immediately remove them from the pan and set aside. When they are cool enough to handle, coarsely chop them.

Trim the ends off the green beans, string them if necessary, and cut them into 1-inch pieces. Heat the oil over medium-high in a large skillet that has a tight-fitting lid. Add the onion and sauté for 1 to 2 minutes. Stir in the green beans and ½ cup of water, cover the pan, and cook for 8 to 10 minutes, until the beans are fork-tender. Remove the lid and cook and stir for 1 to 2 minutes longer, if necessary, until no more than about 1 tablespoon of liquid remains in the pan. Stir in the chiles and crema. Transfer to a warm serving bowl and top with the pumpkin seeds and cilantro. Serve immediately.

Each serving provides:

83	Calories	9 g	Carbohydrate
3 g	Protein	24 mg	Sodium
5 g	Fat	3 mg	Cholesterol
2 g	Dietary Fiber		

Chayotes Braised in Rum

ALMOST INSTANT, VEGAN

Chayotes are a pear-shaped member of the squash family. Seasoned as in this recipe, their flavor is a cross between honeydew melons and cucumbers.

Yield: 6 side-dish servings

Chayotes	2	**medium (about 1 pound)**
Red onion, thinly sliced	½	**medium**
Dark rum	2	**tablespoons**
Fresh oregano leaves, minced	1	**teaspoon**
Salt	¼	**teaspoon**
Pure chile powder	½	**teaspoon**

Cut the chayotes into bite-size cubes, discarding the seed. Slice the red onion. Put the rum and 2 tablespoons of water in a heavy-bottomed skillet that has a tight-fitting lid. Heat over medium heat until steaming, then stir in the chayotes, onion, oregano, salt, and chile powder. Cover the pan and cook 9 to 12 minutes, until the chayotes are just fork-tender, but still a little crisp. Check frequently toward the end of the cooking time and add more water if necessary, 1 tablespoon at a time, replacing the lid and continuing to cook until the chayote is done. Serve hot or warm.

Each serving provides:

32	Calories		5 g	Carbohydrate
1 g	Protein		94 mg	Sodium
0 g	Fat		0 mg	Cholesterol
1 g	Dietary Fiber			

Fried Plantains

Plantains are not really a vegetable, but a member of the banana family. They are marvelous, however, when cooked and served as a vegetable accompaniment to any tortilla or masa dish. Be sure to purchase the plantains well in advance. They are sold when green and need several days to ripen. When ripe, the skin will be uniformly black and the fruit will yield slightly to pressure when gently squeezed.

Yield: 6 side-dish servings

Plantains	**3 large (about 2 pounds)**
Unsalted butter	**2 tablespoons**

Peel the plantains and cut them crosswise at an angle into ½-inch slices. Melt the butter in a large heavy-bottomed skillet over medium-high heat. Add the plantains and cook until golden brown, about 5 minutes. Turn and brown the other sides for 3 to 5 minutes. Serve immediately.

Each serving provides:

134	Calories	26 g	Carbohydrate
1 g	Protein	5 mg	Sodium
4 g	Fat	11 mg	Cholesterol
0 g	Dietary Fiber		

Buttered Beets with Coriander and Lime

Beets continue to be an underappreciated vegetable in the U.S., perhaps because most people are only familiar with canned ones, which do not have the natural sweetness of freshly cooked ones. Here is a delicious way to enjoy these nutritious roots.

Yield: 4 side-dish servings

Small beets, without greens	1	**pound**
Unsalted butter	1	**tablespoon**
Fresh-squeezed lime juice	2	**tablespoons**
Coriander seeds	½	**teaspoon**
Salt	⅛	**teaspoon**
Black pepper		**A few grinds**
Fresh cilantro leaves, minced	2	**tablespoons**

Rinse the beets and place them on a steamer rack in a saucepan that has a tight-fitting lid. Add about 2 inches of water, cover the pan, and cook over medium-high heat about 15 minutes, until each beet can be easily pierced all the way through with a sharp knife (cooking time will vary, depending on the size of the beets). Remove the lid to check the water level midway through the cooking time and add some very hot water, if necessary, to keep the pan from going dry. Set the beets aside in a colander to cool for several minutes.

Crush the coriander seeds thoroughly with a mortar and pestle. When the beets are cool enough to handle (but still quite warm), slip off and discard the skins. Cut the beets into bite-size chunks. Toss the beets with the butter, lime juice, coriander seeds, salt, and pepper in a warmed serving bowl. Distribute the cilantro leaves over the top, and serve.

Each serving provides:

69	Calories	10 g	Carbohydrate
2 g	Protein	135 mg	Sodium
3 g	Fat	8 mg	Cholesterol
2 g	Dietary Fiber		

Fresh Greens with Tomatoes, Garlic, and Cumin

ALMOST INSTANT, VEGAN

Any favorite leafy green could be used for this dish. We like the more bitter varieties—such as collards and mustard greens—because their flavors stand up well beside spicy main dishes. Any combination of your favorite greens is fine here.

Yield: 4 side-dish servings

Fresh collard greens	**2**	**pounds**
Canned whole tomatoes, drained and chopped	**1**	**28-ounce can**
Garlic	**2**	**cloves, minced**
Ground cumin	**1½**	**teaspoons**
Granulated sugar	**½**	**teaspoon**
Salt	**¼**	**teaspoon**
Black pepper		**Several grinds**
Fresh-squeezed lime juice	**2**	**tablespoons**

Carefully wash and dry the greens, discarding any tough stems. chop the greens coarsely. Set aside.

Place the tomatoes, garlic, cumin, sugar, salt, and pepper in a large stockpot and bring to a simmer over medium-high heat. Pile the greens on top of the tomato sauce and cover the pan.

Cook 10 minutes, then remove the lid, add the lime juice, and stir to combine the greens with the sauce. Transfer to a warmed serving bowl. Serve hot.

Each serving provides:

73	Calories	16 g	Carbohydrate
4 g	Protein	511 mg	Sodium
1 g	Fat	0 mg	Cholesterol
2 g	Dietary Fiber		

Sautéed Zucchini and Corn with Chipotle Chiles

ALMOST INSTANT

This simple preparation relies on the crunchy flavor of fresh zucchini and corn. We enjoy serving it as soon as fresh corn shows up in the markets. Add more chile if you enjoy food that is really spicy.

Yield: 4 side-dish servings

Zucchini	3	**medium (1 pound)**
Fresh corn	2	**medium ears**
Unsalted butter	1	**tablespoon**
Yellow onion, diced	½	**cup**
Chipotle chiles en adobo, minced	1	**teaspoon**

Remove and discard the stem ends from the zucchini. Slice the zucchini in half lengthwise, then cut each half in half again lengthwise. Then chop crosswise into ½-inch pieces and set aside. Cut the corn from cob to measure about 1 cup. Set the corn aside.

Melt the butter in a heavy-bottomed skillet over medium-high heat and add the zucchini and onion. Cook, stirring frequently, about 3 minutes, then add the corn. Continue to cook, stirring occasionally, for about 8 minutes, until the zucchini is just fork-tender. Stir in the chile, heat through for about 1 minute, then serve hot or at room temperature.

Each serving provides:

90	Calories	15 g	Carbohydrate
2 g	Protein	13 mg	Sodium
4 g	Fat	8 mg	Cholesterol
3 g	Dietary Fiber		

Potato Cakes with Corn and Queso Fresco

Fresh corn is preferred for this dish because it adds a nice crunch, but if it is not in season, you may substitute frozen corn. Serve these cakes as an interesting side dish with enchiladas, or for breakfast with salsa and fresh fruit. This recipe makes 12 to 15 (3-inch) cakes.

Yield: 6 side-dish servings

Russet potatoes	1	pound (about 2 large)
Fresh Anaheim chile	1	medium (about ¼ pound)
Olive oil	2	tablespoons
Garlic	2	cloves, minced
Yellow onion	1	small, diced
Corn kernels, fresh or frozen*	1	cup
Pure chile powder	½	teaspoon
Ground cumin	¼	teaspoon
Salt	⅛	teaspoon
Green onions	2	medium, minced
Part-skim queso fresco, crumbled	3	ounces (about ¾ cup)

Scrub and dice the potatoes. Place them in a medium saucepan, cover with water, and bring to a boil. Once boiling, cook for 8 to 10 minutes, until fork-tender. Drain the potatoes well, transfer to a bowl, and mash them thoroughly.

*If using fresh corn, you will need about 2 medium ears to yield 1 cup kernels.

Meanwhile, remove and discard the stem end and seeds from the chile and finely dice it. Heat 1 tablespoon of the olive oil over medium heat in a large skillet and add the garlic and yellow onion. Sauté for about 1 minute, then stir in the chile, corn, chile powder, cumin, and salt. Sauté, stirring frequently, for about 5 minutes.

Stir the sautéed vegetables into the potatoes, along with the green onions and cheese. Form the mixture into 3-inch patties. Lightly coat the bottom of the skillet with some of the remaining 1 tablespoon oil and heat it over medium-high heat. Fill the skillet with potato cakes and cook them until golden brown, about 5 minutes, then turn and brown the other side, 3 to 5 minutes. Place cooked cakes on a serving platter and keep them warm while you cook the remaining cakes, adding a bit of oil to the skillet as necessary. If using a well-seasoned cast-iron skillet, you should need no more than a total of 2 tablespoons oil.

Each serving provides:

208	Calories	30 g	Carbohydrate
7 g	Protein	149 mg	Sodium
8 g	Fat	8 mg	Cholesterol
3 g	Dietary Fiber		

Roasted Potatoes and Shallots with Oregano

VEGAN

Oven-roasted potatoes have a crispy outside but a melt-in-your-mouth inside. The shallots and oregano are perfect flavor complements. Drizzle with Lowfat Crema (page 34), if desired.

Yield: 6 side-dish servings

Small red or white potatoes	2	**pounds**
Shallots	½	**pound**
Olive oil	2	**tablespoons**
Dried Mexican oregano	1	**teaspoon**
Pure chile powder	¼	**teaspoon**
Salt	⅛	**teaspoon**
Black pepper		**Several grinds**

Preheat the oven to 375 degrees F. Rinse the potatoes, or scrub them if they are dirty. Without peeling them, cut the potatoes into 1-inch cubes. Peel the shallots and separate them into individual cloves, or chop them into 1-inch pieces if they are large. Place the potatoes and shallots in a bowl and drizzle with the olive oil. Toss with a wooden spoon to coat. Add the oregano, chile powder, salt, and pepper and toss again. Transfer to a large casserole dish or a high-walled baking sheet. Bake for about 45 minutes, until the potatoes are fork-tender. Toss or stir them occasionally during the cooking time. Remove to a warm platter and serve immediately.

Each serving provides:

224	Calories	43 g	Carbohydrate
4 g	Protein	60 mg	Sodium
5 g	Fat	0 mg	Cholesterol
2 g	Dietary Fiber		

Potatoes Baked in Salsa Verde with Cheese

Potatoes are humble and hearty and appreciated both north and south of the border. This dish combines sliced potatoes with a green sauce and melted cheese for a dish substantial and tasty enough to serve as a main course; it also makes a delicious side dish for any light Mexican entrée.

Yield: 6 main-dish servings

White or red potatoes	2½	**pounds**
Fresh tomatillos	1½	**pounds (18 medium)**
Fresh cilantro leaves	1	**cup**
Canned whole mild green chiles	1	**4-ounce can**
Green onions	6	**medium, minced**
Garlic	2	**cloves, minced**
Mexican Vegetable Stock°	1	**cup**
Salt	½	**teaspoon**
Granulated sugar	½	**teaspoon**
Canola oil	1	**tablespoon plus ½ teaspoon**
Muenster cheese, shredded	8	**ounces (2 cups)**

°If you do not have Mexican Vegetable Stock on hand, make a batch according to the directions on page 38, or dissolve ½ large low-sodium vegetable broth cube in 1 cup of hot water.

Preheat the oven to 375 degrees F. Scrub the potatoes and, without peeling them, cut crosswise into ¼-inch slices. Bring 1 inch of water to a boil in a small saucepan. Insert a steamer rack in the pan and place the potato slices on the rack. Cover the pan and steam the potatoes about 8 minutes, until barely fork-tender. They will finish cooking in the oven. Immediately remove the potatoes from the pan and set them aside in a colander at room temperature.

Meanwhile, peel off and discard the papery husks of the tomatillos. Rinse the tomatillos and place them in a saucepan with 1 cup of water. Cover and cook over medium-high heat 7 minutes, until the tomatillos are very soft. Drain briefly and transfer the tomatillos to a blender. Add the cilantro, chiles, green onions, garlic, stock, salt, and sugar to the blender and purée thoroughly. Heat the 1 tablespoon oil in a heavy-bottomed skillet over medium heat and strain the purée through a fine mesh strainer into the pan, pressing with the back of a wooden spoon to force everything but the seeds through the mesh. Bring to a simmer and cook for 5 minutes, stirring frequently.

(continued)

Rub the remaining ½ teaspoon oil on the bottom and sides of a 2-quart baking dish. Spread ½ cup of the sauce over the bottom of the baking dish and place half of the potatoes in an even layer on top of the sauce. Top with half of the cheese and half of the remaining sauce. Repeat the layers, ending with sauce. Shake the dish gently to settle the contents. Bake, covered, for 25 minutes, then remove the lid and bake for 20 minutes longer, until the top is slightly browned. Allow to stand in the baking dish at room temperature for at least 5 minutes before serving.

Each serving provides:

409	Calories	56 g	Carbohydrate
15 g	Protein	611 mg	Sodium
15 g	Fat	36 mg	Cholesterol
4 g	Dietary Fiber		

Sources of Mexican Ingredients

Many large supermarket chains carry the basic ingredients of Mexican cooking, including masa harina, canned and pickled chiles, and specialty produce. In addition, many communities in the U.S. have grocery stores that cater to the Mexican population. At these markets, you will find everything you need to enjoy cooking in the Mexican style. To locate them, consult the yellow pages of your telephone book under groceries and/or tortilla factories.

If you don't have a local source for certain ingredients, you may be able to obtain them through mail-order companies, such as the ones listed below.

Colorado Spice Company
5030 Nome Street
Denver, CO 80239
303/373-9215

This company sells a vast selection of dried herbs and spices by mail, as well as some canned and bottled products, such as hot sauces.

Coyote Cucina Catalog
1364 Rufina Circle #1
Santa Fe, MN 87501
800/866-HOWL

The premier southwestern restaurant of Santa Fe also has a general store and an extensive mail-order food catalog.

Don Alfonso Foods
P.O. Box 201988
Austin, TX 78720
800/456-6100

This company offers its own brand of cooking sauces and salsas by mail, as well as dried chiles and chile powders and some Mexican specialty equipment, such as tortilla presses.

Stonewall Chili Pepper Co.
Highway 290, Box 241
Stonewall, TX
800/232-2995

This chile pepper growing operation sells dried chiles and related products, such as salsas and jellies.

Index

O

Oils and butter
   about, 13–14
Okra, Corn chowder with ancho chiles,
   and cream, 142
Olive(s)
   Potato, zucchini, and, stew with garlic,
      jalapeños, and tomatoes, 153
Olive oil, about, 13
Omelet
   Baked green chile and cheese, 242
   Baked tortilla, with spinach, cilantro,
      and green chiles, 244
   Baked tortilla, with zucchini and
      mushrooms, 246
Onion(s)
   about, 8–9
   browned, Pasta with, cauliflower,
      serrano chile, and mint, 276
   cilantro, and serrano relish, 65
   Simple refritos with, and oregano, 286
Orange(s)
   about, 7–8
   anise dressing, Romaine and radish
      salad with, 124
   dressing, Cauliflower corn salad
      with, 108
   lime marinade, Jicama and cucumber
      salad with, 106
Oregano. *See also* Mexican oregano.
   Pickled vegetables and serrano chiles
      with, and thyme, 58
   Roasted potatoes and shallots
      with, 322
   Simple refritos with onion and, 286

P

Panela cheese, about, 2
Pantry, Stocking the, 1–17
Pasta
   about, 14, 252–253
   salad with grilled vegetables and
      roasted garlic dressing, 118
   tips and tools, 253–254
Pasta Dishes, Rice and. *See* Contents for
   list of recipe titles.
Pastina, Spinach and corn soup with, and
   smoked cheese, 138
Peas
   Red rice with, 258
Peanut(s)
   about, 12

Roasted, with chile and lime juice, 84
Pepper(s). *Also see* Chile(s).
   red bell, Jicama and, plate, 96
   Roasted, black bean, and avocado
      tacos with bleu cheese, 174
   roasted, Burritos with spinach,
      artichokes, and feta cheese, 180
   roasted red bell, Spinach salad with
      spiced walnuts and, 122
   tequila-sautéed, Cream soup with, and
      fresh tomato, 140
Pesto, cilantro, Pasta with, and
   avocado, 274
Pickled
   eggs with Mexican spices, 230
   vegetables and serrano chiles with
      oregano and thyme, 66
Pickled jalapeño(s) chiles
   Nachos with beans and, 90
   Nopalito salad with, 110
   Soft tacos with tofu and, 170
Pineapple, Lentil stew with, and
   banana, 156
Pinto beans
   Burritos with potatoes, and
      guacamole, 182
   in Basic pot beans, 284
   in Nachos with beans and pickled
      jalapeños, 90
   in Simple refritos with onion and
      oregano, 286
   Whole, with minced vegetables, 292
   Yellow rice and, 266
Plantain(s)
   about, 8
   filling, savory, Empanadas with, 70
   Fried, 313
Poached, Eggs, in garlic tomato sauce
   with chile strips and cheese, 240
Poblano chile(s)
   about, 5
   and cinnamon sauce, Pasta
      with, 270
   Chard and, enchiladas with tomatillo
      sauce, 197
   Green tomato salsa with, 50
   Masa casserole with corn, zucchini,
      and, 218
   Tortillas with cheese, cinnamon, and
      cumin, 92
Potato(es)
   and chorizo tacos, 178

Scrambled eggs with, and
potatoes, 234
Tomato(es). *See also* Tomato(es),
cherry.
about, 16
Avocado, bisque, 132
Baked rice with black beans, corn,
and epazote, 268
Eggs scrambled with green beans
and tomatoes, 236
fresh corn, and cilantro salsa, 52
fresh, Cream soup with tequila-
sautéed peppers and, 140
Fresh greens with, garlic, and
cumin, 316
garlic, sauce, Eggs poached in, with
chile strips and cheese, 240
Green, salsa with poblano chiles, 50
in Salsa cruda, 54
in Salsa fresca, 56
Marinated garbanzo beans with
roasted garlic, and capers, 294
Nopalito and, quesadillas, 76
Nopalitos with zucchini, and
eggs, 232
Potato, zucchini, and olive stew with
garlic, jalapeños, and, 153
Pumpkin seed tamales filled with
eggs, greens, and tomatoes, 205
red, Tomatillo salsa with, and
zucchini, 48
Rice and garbanzo soup with
chipotle chiles, avocado, and, 144
sauce, creamy spiced, Pasta and
broccoli with, 278
sauce, grilled, Corn and cheese
tortilla casserole with, 200
sauce, grilled, Pasta with, 272
sauce, serrano chile, Lima beans and
mushrooms in, 298
Scrambled eggs with green beans
and, 236
soup with fideos and serrano
chiles, 136
White beans with, and serrano
chiles, 296
Tomato(es), cherry
salad with green onions and
cilantro, 104
Tortilla(s)
casserole, Corn and cheese, with
grilled tomato sauce, 200

chip salad with lime shallot
dressing, 116
corn, Fresh, 42
heating, 30
omelet, Baked, with spinach,
cilantro, and green onions, 244
omelet, Baked with zucchini and
mushrooms, 246
strips, fried, Vegetable soup with,
and avocado salsa, 150
with cheese, poblano chiles,
cinnamon, and cumin, 92
Tortilla Dishes. *See* Contents for list of
recipe titles.
about, 158–159
tips and tools, 159–160
Tostadas
Refried beans and chorizo, 168
with roasted nopalitos, 166

V
Vegan recipe index, xxx
Vegetable(s)
Grilled, and rice burritos, 184
grilled, Pasta salad with, and roasted
garlic dressing, 118
minced, Whole pinto beans
with, 292
Pickled, and serrano chiles with
oregano and thyme, 66
soup with fried tortilla strips and
avocado salsa, 150
stock, Mexican, 38
Vegetable Side Dishes, Hot. *See*
Contents for list of recipe titles.
about, 300–301
tips and tools, 301
Vinaigrette, Mexicali, Leafy greens
with cabbage and, 120

W
Walnut(s)
spiced, Spinach salad with, and
roasted red bell pepper, 122
White beans with tomatoes and
serrano chiles, 296
Winter squash. *See* Acorn squash.

Y
Yam, Split pea soup with, and Mexican
seasonings, 146